WRITERS AND CRITICS

WILLIAM GOLDING

LEIGHTON HODSON

CAPRICORN BOOKS
NEW YORK

CAPRICORN BOOKS EDITION, 1971

Published by arrangement with
OLIVER AND BOYD LTD.
Tweeddale Court, Edinburgh 1

First published 1969

Library of Congress Catalog
Card Number: 77-172990

Printed in the United States of America

CONTENTS

ACKNOWLEDGMENTS

Thanks are due to Mr William Golding and Professor Frank Kermode for permission to quote from their BBC Third Programme discussion of 28 Aug. 1959.

The photograph on the front cover is reproduced by permission of Cameta Press.

ABBREVIATED TITLES BY WHICH GOLDING'S WORKS ARE CITED IN REFERENCES

L.F.	=	*Lord of the Flies.*
T.I.	=	*The Inheritors.*
P.M.	=	*Pincher Martin.*
B.B.	=	*The Brass Butterfly.*
F.F.	=	*Free Fall.*
T.S.	=	*The Spire.*
H.G.	=	*The Hot Gates.*
T.P.	=	*The Pyramid.*

CHAPTER I

BIOGRAPHICAL INTRODUCTION

William Gerald Golding was born at St Columb Minor, near Newquay in Cornwall, on 19 Sept. 1911. His father, Alec Golding, was a schoolmaster and author of a standard school geography. It was a family of schoolmasters and in his turn William Golding too became one. Yet his intention in life was to be a writer—a poet, really—though it was not until the publication of his first novel, *Lord of the Flies*, in 1954, that he emerged having achieved his intention and, at the same time, complete mastery of his craft. In spite of great achievements since that date it is this work, and the film made from it, that have left their mark on the general public. There are, no doubt, many reasons why; chief among these are its great readability, if only as a narrative, and the frightening power of its content. It caught, too, the post-war mood for an examination of the inalienable violence in human nature and the need to meditate on it. It was completely different from the novels of satirical comment on the often comic niceties of snobbish class barriers in British life and, for all its particular subject, it was universal in a way that psychological novels rarely are. It had the quality of striking at the heart like poetry.

As a novelist Golding made his début, therefore, with a masterpiece, but at the age of forty-three. If there was silence in the creative field until 1954 it was for the austere reason that Golding was not satisfied with novels insufficiently marked by his own personality. By 1954 he had written three novels which remained unpublished because he considered them derivative. He felt he was writing other people's books while what he wanted to say needed a new story.[1] He has also said that he sees the novel as a unique pattern that should not be repeated to order:

> It seems to me that there's really very little point in writing a novel unless you do something that either you suspected you couldn't do, or which you are pretty certain nobody else has tried before. I don't think there's any point in writing two books that are like each other.[2]

This helps to explain the technical complexity of his remaining novels: *The Inheritors* (1955), *Pincher Martin* (1956), *Free Fall* (1959), *The Spire* (1964), and *The Pyramid* (1967). It suggests, too, why all his novels except his first have proved difficult reading and lost him a truly popular following in spite of their excellence. Though not an experimentalist in the novel like James Joyce, Virginia Woolf or the writers of the *nouveau roman*, Golding has always taken great trouble to find a form for his work that corresponds to and illuminates his subject. Form and content with him are welded together as they are in poetry.

This quality of poetry fills Golding's fiction whether in the symbolic richness of his themes or in the intricacy and suggestiveness of his descriptions. It is not surprising to find that his first publication was a book of poems, the first public expression of the urge to write that he seems to have had from the age of seven.[3] His *Poems* (1934) were a slim volume of twenty-nine short lyrics which he is now glad to abandon to oblivion. Indeed, he says so in no uncertain terms and has told one interviewer that he

[1] See O. Webster, "Living with chaos", *Books and Art*, Mar. 1958, p. 15.

[2] F. Kermode, Interview with Golding for BBC, 28 Aug. 1959.

[3] See J. W. Aldridge, "William Golding", *New York Times Book Review*, 10 Dec. 1961, p. 56.

does not own a copy.[4] He treats the matter more lightly, however, and in a tone that is self-mocking, in an essay called "Crosses". Rather more important to him among the little irritants and crosses of his life is the one he describes as his inability to write poetry:

> I remember the awe with which I contemplated my first finished set of verses and thought it was a poem . . . When I was twenty-one, a friend sent my verses to a publisher who in a moment of blindness offered to publish them . . . I wondered how big my fanmail would be.
>
> Of course, nothing happened at all. The little book was not even reviewed . . . Well, I went on writing verses . . . and got together another book. But there came the day, and I can only suppose it was the day on which I grew up, when I saw my verses for the poor, thin things they were . . .[5]

This gives us a picture of Golding as a rather more humorous person than the serious atmosphere of his novels has suggested to most people. It is also obvious that, on the question of poetry and prose, he is really very deeply involved. This comes over, too, in his answer to an observation concerning the poetic quality of his prose and its tendency almost to become poetry. To his interviewer he says:

> . . . Ah, you see you said *almost*. But not quite. And it's not poetry because I write prose. The novelist is a displaced person, torn between two ways of expression. . . . You might say I write prose because I can't write poetry.[6]

What is betrayed here is Golding's exceptional deter-

[4] See B. Dick, "The novelist is a displaced person. An interview with William Golding", *College English*, Mar. 1965, p. 480.

[5] *H.G.*, p. 27.

[6] Dick, *op. cit.*, p. 480.

mination to mature as an artistic personality before finally committing himself to print. His writing, in spite of his disclaimer, aspires naturally to the condition of poetry. His great belief in the twenty years between the publication of the *Poems* and *Lord of the Flies* is that the man, and not the writer, must be made first.[7] Golding spent these twenty years doing adult teaching. This included travelling widely over the country and lecturing in Maidstone Gaol and army camps. He was also, for a while, part-time actor, writer, and producer for a small provincial theatre company, one of his acting roles being Danny in Emlyn Williams's *Night Must Fall*.[8] With World War II he became a sailor and served with the Royal Navy. He spent most of the War at sea and ended up as Lieutenant of a rocket-launcher. He saw action on numerous occasions and was involved in the sinking of the *Bismarck* and in the landings in Normandy on D-day.[9]

He is able now to look back on his literary development during that period and laugh at himself. In "It's a long way to Oxyrhynchus" he describes in a humorous way his determination to write while at the same time finding no one willing to publish him:

> When I have tried every publisher there is and still been turned down, and am still haunted by this desperate, cruel, bloody business of believing I can write —when all ways are blocked, I can think of one left. I shall take my MSS aboard a boat. I shall go to Egypt. I shall get up the Nile to Oxyrhynchus, walk into the dumb, dry desert and bury the lot next to the city rubbish tip. In AD 5000 they will be excavated by Pekin University, and published among the seven hundred and fifty volumes of *Vestiges of Western Literature*. Of course no one will read them, any more than

[7] See Aldridge, *op. cit.*, p. 56.
[8] See *H.G.*, p. 126; Dick, *op. cit.*, p. 480; Aldridge, *op. cit.*, p. 56.
[9] See *H.G.*, p. 42; Aldridge, *op. cit.*, p. 56.

they read Erinna or Bacchylides. This obsession with writing is pointless as alcoholism and there's no Authors Anonymous to wean you from the typewriter.[10]

It seems that the tasks he set himself at this time were in particular the writing of parodies. He describes parody very wittily in this essay as depending "on the mean advantage of being wise after someone else's event", and gives three examples of his ability as a parodist. He half-makes fun of Mauriac, C. S. Forester, and Shakespeare but manages also to blend into his parodies a strain of his own character.

It is not so surprising to find the tendency to use parody culminating in his first successful work, *Lord of the Flies*, which has Ballantyne's *The Coral Island* as its starting point. However, this is no longer parody with affection; it's as if, in turning to attack and invert his new victim, he has discovered himself. Golding's long concern with writing parodies for his own amusement has produced an upsurge of original thought and writing. The process of parodying has been catalytic, in the sense that, given authors and works whose ingrained and stodgy opinions he is compelled to disagree with, he has been able by inverting them to discover his own style. He has left his victims well behind him and has raced ahead to recreate a view of the human condition that modern readers can recognise.

Any reader of Golding soon becomes aware of how, beneath the vigorous and idiosyncratic surface of his novels, there steams a compost of childhood and adolescent reading from which the new growth derives its force. Golding's reading lay first among the Victorian adventure-story writers like Ballantyne and Henty and later Wells, Poe, Jules Verne, and a considerable amount of Science Fiction. He has described how he has found the Victorian story-tellers puerile and Jules Verne some-

[10] In *Spectator*, 7 Jul. 1961, p. 9.

thing of a dead loss.[11] Science Fiction, though he has enjoyed it well enough, is only a game and perhaps a bit of a time-waster in spite of the fact that he has indulged in it for forty years. The "play" side of Science Fiction does appeal to him in lighter moods: "I have to confess . . . to a basic irresponsibility which enables me to make a sharp division between myself as a pint-sized Jeremiah and myself just frivolously *sent* by the dexterity of what goes on", *i.e.* in Science Fiction.[12] He has, in fact, collaborated on a volume of short stories called *Sometime, Never—Three Tales of Imagination* (1956). His own contribution, "Envoy Extraordinary", makes fun of modern inventions, including a steamship, explosives, printing, and a pressure cooker, "advanced" to the time of Imperial Rome. This was later reworked as the play, *The Brass Butterfly* (1958).

Undoubtedly, an important ingredient in the personality of the later artist was his childhood reading, particularly of juvenile literature, and his rejection of its simplistic views on contact with the world of maturity. He says that he has "a pretty well defined library behind me in childhood to explain the size of my mind and its mental furniture".[13] Only the adult reader can become aware of what the child reader was oblivious of: the satire of Swift, the evangelism of Bunyan, even the loneliness in *Robinson Crusoe*.[14]

Literature is an obsessional study with him. At first it seemed that his path would go in the completely opposite direction, in the direction of science. He received his secondary education at Marlborough Grammar School, Wiltshire, where his father was Senior Assistant Master, and in 1930, at the age of nineteen, he went up to Brasenose College, Oxford. He at first read science to

[11] See "Astronaut by Gaslight" in *H.G.*, pp. 111-15.
[12] "Androids All", *Spectator*, 24 Feb. 1961.
[13] BBC Interview with Golding.
[14] See *H.G.*, p. 111.

please his father but in two years he was convinced that his real interests were literary. He decided to change to studying English Literature and took particular interest in Anglo-Saxon. He graduated in 1935 and also studied for a Diploma in Education. Among his literary influences in the positive sense, as opposed to books he had read as a child or adolescent, only to reject, he includes the Anglo-Saxon epic poem *The Battle of Maldon* and Greek Literature, especially Homer and Euripides.

His liking for *The Battle of Maldon*,[15] a poem written towards the end of the tenth century and notable for its stoic theme of resistance against the Danes, suggests Golding's growing predilection for the sombre in literature, the sombre but at the same time the noble. His other main literary obsession, the study of Greek, he began in order to help pass the hours of the watch while he was in the Navy during the War. He communicates his enthusiasm for Greece in his essay called "The Hot Gates", the eponymous essay of a collection of occasional pieces published in 1965. In general, they range over his many interests from literature, archaeology, travel, and teaching to reminiscences of childhood. "The Hot Gates" itself recaptures the atmosphere of Thessaly, describes his visit to the Pass of Thermopylae, and celebrates the stand of Leonidas and his three hundred Spartans, in the name of freedom, against the vast army of Xerxes. He describes his climb up the cliffs and is anxious to convey the physical intimacy of his attachment to Greece:

> I stayed there, clinging to a rock. . . . Suddenly, the years and the reading fused with the thing. I was clinging to Greece herself.[16]

Even more than with his admiration for *The Battle of Maldon* he speaks, in his admiration of Leonidas, of the thrill of stoical resistance combined with the defence of

[15] See A. T. Broes, *Lectures on Modern Novelists*, Pittsburgh, 1963, pp. 1-14.
[16] *H.G.*, p. 19.

liberty. The courage and determination to face evil will, in fact, be noticeable as a recurring theme of his own work:

> ... that company stood in the right line of history. A little of Leonidas lies in the fact that I can go where I like and write what I like. He contributed to set us free.[17]

He communicates likewise his enthusiasm for the Greek language in a review of a translation of Homer. Far better, in his opinion, would be to read Homer in the original. For Golding learning Greek is no trouble at all, and in any case an adult learner has the repeated phrases like "rosy-fingered dawn" coming round every so often to help him.[18] No translation can take the place for him of prime contact with the Greek authors. For fifteen years after the War he preferred to read nothing but classical Greek mainly because this is where he thought the meat was.[19] He has particular admiration for Euripides. Though influence in any naive sense must be ruled out there is undeniably a sympathy in atmosphere between Greek tragedy and Golding's outlook, especially with reference to *The Bacchae*, Euripides' last play, which he knows inside out.[20] It is grim but also touching in its theme. Agave in her madness, as agent of Dionysus, murders her son, Pentheus, who had rationally but stubbornly attempted to deny the god. So passions denied revenge themselves on reason, but once spent are themselves bereft, as Agave, having returned to her senses, is left to acknowledge and mourn the murder of her son. The implications of this theme underlie and illustrate a basic preoccupation of Golding's. There is a

[17] *Op. cit.*, p. 20.
[18] "Surge and Thunder", *Spectator*, 14 Sep. 1962.
[19] See D. M. Davis, "A Conversation with Golding", *The New Republic*, 4 May 1963, p. 30.
[20] See Dick, *op. cit.*, p. 481.

balance between reason and the passions, mind and sentiment, that it is foolish for humanity to ignore. The whole truth is with neither side—passions in the ascendancy lead to violence and suffering; reason in the ascendancy is bound to fail human nature since the unruly passions must bubble up. This is reflected in varying subtle ways in the novels against a wide background of human experience, and the tragic thing that is illuminated is the general unwillingness to admit a failing on one side or the other. To put it in a necessarily over-simple way, Jack and his choir in *Lord of the Flies* are opposed to the steady-minded Ralph and Piggy; in *The Inheritors* the rational has helped the new men to develop techniques of oppression against the Neanderthalers; Pincher Martin threshes heroically about in his passions but is finally proved wrong however vigorous his spirit; Sammy in *Free Fall* has always placed his passions and desires before any fair attempt to understand other people; Jocelin in *The Spire* appears to live by his own reason and determination when all is, in fact, founded upon self-deception and emotional dishonesty: finally, Oliver in *The Pyramid* sees the truth behind lives that are crippled or destroyed by unhealthy repressiveness.

By right, it might appear that reason, man's prime and distinguishing attribute, should solve his problems. Yet frequently in the novels Golding attacks the reliance on the rational alone as if it were a safe answer to human failings and torments. This reflects his own decision to leave the study of science for the pursuit of the arts, and, in an essay on education called "On the Crest of the Wave", he makes out his case for the greater value overall of the arts to modern man. This is not just a personal choice of what he happens to like but a real belief in the necessity of the arts if we are to preserve our humanity:

> Our humanity rests in the capacity to make value judgments, unscientific assessments, the power to

decide that this is right, that wrong, this ugly, that beautiful, this just, that unjust. Yet these are precisely the questions which "Science" is not qualified to answer with its measurement and analysis. They can be answered only by the methods of philosophy and the arts.[21]

The man of science Golding admires is Copernicus, precisely for his blending of scientific enquiry with imagination and intuition.[22] In modern times the example Golding prefers is a seer like Rudolf Steiner even though seers have all the odds against them. Unlike the thinkers of vision in past ages Steiner's seership belonged to the nineteenth and twentieth centuries and so was destined for a direct clash with rationalism. Though Steiner came out of it badly and was treated rather contemptuously Golding is impressed by the relevance of what Steiner attempted to our present times:

But today Steiner cannot be got rid of so easily. To begin with, there is a deep desire in the minds of people to break out of the globe of their own skulls, and find the significance in the cosmos that mere measurement misses. Any man who claims to have found a bridge between the world of the physical sciences and the world of the spirit is sure of a hearing. Is this not because most of us have an unexpressed faith that the bridge exists, even if we have not the wit to discover it?[23]

In 1939 Golding had married and settled down as a

[21] *H.G.*, p. 130.

[22] *Op. cit.*, pp. 31-40. *Cf.* "Thin Partitions", *Spectator*, 13 Jan. 1961; a review of *Some Reflections on Genius and Other Essays* by Russell Brain, 1961. Golding is not over-impressed by the attempt to nail down genius with medical terminology; scientific labelling is no virtue in itself.

[23] "All or Nothing", *Spectator*, 24 Mar. 1961; review of *The Faithful Thinker*, ed. A. C. Harwood, 1961. Centenary essays on Rudolf Steiner.

schoolmaster at Bishop Wordsworth's School, Salisbury. The War was to interrupt his career there though he returned in 1945 and taught English and Philosophy. The experiences of the War and the picture of the world that it fostered seem to have been crucial. He has said that World War II was the turning-point for him when he began to see what people were capable of doing.[24] He insists, on the question of Good and Evil in his work, that his intentions are simply to analyse the motives of human behaviour, even though his view of that behaviour has been darkened by his experience of violence and war:

> I'm not saying anyone is evil. I set out to discover whether there is that in man which makes him do what he does, that's all. When I was young, before the War, I did have some airy-fairy views about man, though I wasn't a Marxist (you'll find, I think, that the Marxists are the only people left who think humanity is perfectible). But I went through the War and that changed me. The war taught me different and a lot of others like me.[25]

There is an anecdote that seems to illustrate Golding's dilemma over the ambivalence of his war experiences:

> On one occasion a nervous tic, produced by stress and hazard, twisted his face into what appeared to be a wide grin of bloodthirsty elation. As the danger increased the grin grew even wider until, finally, his awe-struck men began whispering to one another: "Look at the Old Man. Regular fire-eater he is. The hotter it gets, the better he likes it." When the tension at last left the Golding facial muscles, the grin disappeared but was immediately replaced by an equally uncontrollable expression of acute bereavement:

[24] See J. Wershba, "William Golding", *New York Post*, 17 Dec. 1963, p. 31.

[25] Davis, *op. cit.*, p. 28.

"Look at the Old Man now", said his men, "See how he hates it when we get out of danger. Regular fire-eater he is."[26]

The experience of life during the War and after began to correspond in its harshness to the kind of literature Golding had come to admire. He sums up his point of view succinctly when he writes:

> I am by nature an optimist; but a defective logic—or a logic which I sometimes hope desperately is defective—makes a pessimist of me.[27]

And so it is a natural outcome of this that he should create *Lord of the Flies*, a novel he wrote purely to please himself, which deals with the harshness and bitterness of existence while yet revealing the potential nobility of the human spirit. The severity of *Lord of the Flies* was matched by its understanding and humanity, and these qualities troubled, impressed and inspired his first readers. Golding was made a Fellow of The Royal Society of Literature in 1955 and he was to receive further honours in 1966 when he was awarded the C.B.E.

He continued teaching at Bishop Wordsworth's School until 1961 and then went for a year as writer-in-residence to Hollins College, Virginia, a rich girls' college, in the Alleghanies.[28] He has evoked the quiet, peace, and dreaminess of Virginia, with its colour problem, for the moment only sleepily brooding on the margin of life there. On the other hand, being jetted around the United States on lecture tours and visits presented a contrast. The body was being delivered to its various destinations long before the soul could catch up with it.[29] As a teacher his concern, of course, was with creative writing, and though he feels driven to mock its ludicrous sides he is prepared to admit the usefulness of such classes

[26] Aldridge, *op. cit.*, p. 56.
[27] *H.G.*, p. 126.
[28] *Op. cit.*, p. 140.
[29] *Op. cit.*, pp. 145-51.

for some people.[30] In general American undergraduate students seem to him eager but too content with a "digest" attitude to their study of literature.[31]

Since 1962 Golding has devoted himself solely to his writing. He lives in his four-hundred-year-old thatched cottage near Salisbury and spends his spare time on his many hobbies—archaeology, Egyptology, classical Greek, music—he is a competent musician and plays the piano, violin, viola, cello, and oboe—and on sailing. His converted fishing-smack, in which in 1967 he was hoping to sail to Greece, capsized after a collision in the English Channel off the Isle of Wight. The incident recalls his wary opinion of the Channel in an essay on navigation. He describes this vast water, so dangerous for small boats, where disaster is always at hand:

> A boat simply disappears. One was a boatload of Sea Scouts, an experienced crew with an experienced officer in charge. Last year a large ketch vanished—no one knows how, though you may guess. Somewhere in the hooting and whining gloom a high, steel bow cracked open and cut down a wooden box, unseeing, unknowing, and passed on . . .[32]

Golding may well have remembered these remarks in the summer of 1967; luckily, all passengers and crew were saved though the Channel took the boat.

It is the nautical side of him that has generally impressed in descriptions of his appearance. He is described as "an astute well-feasted Viking in full beard"[33] or "looking like a nautical Moses".[34] The descriptions clash only in the suggestion of extrovert wanderer in one and introvert prophet in the other. But in manner Golding has given the impression of gentleness, even shyness. He does not seek out publicity and has only

[30] *Op. cit.*, pp. 152-6.
[31] See Davis, *op. cit.*, p. 29.
[32] *H.G.*, p. 45.
[33] Aldridge, *op. cit.*, p. 56.
[34] Dick, *op. cit.*, p. 480.

rarely given interviews of a personal nature. In the essays he provides some engaging details of his appearance. He was unwilling even as a boy to have his unruly hair cut, and the same applies now to his beard.[35] He gives an impression of himself as a child of eight in "Billy the Kid"[36]: a tough fair-haired boy with eyes blue as cornflowers whose first experience of school, as it has been for so many others, was as an outlet for fights. When not fighting his pastime was inventing lists of words.

He spent practically the whole of his life, until he was a young man, in the family home in Marlborough—a house of three slumped storeys of medieval origin next to the graveyard of St Mary's Church. It was a lower middleclass milieu something similar to the setting for his latest novel, *The Pyramid.* In Golding's case the background was the world of teachers and forthright radical opinions like support for Votes for Women. His mother, Mildred Golding, was in the local suffragette movement and actively supported by her husband. He describes his background, in a very revealing and interesting autobiographical essay called "The Ladder and the Tree", as poor and respectable. Even in later manhood the family was still extremely poor and he never had a study or the uxury of silence in which to write.[37]

He brings out, in the picture of his childhood, the striking contrasts between the happiness of the family circle with his mother, father, and brother and the brooding imagination of a child's memories of the graveyard next door and of the, to him, ominous darkness of the cellars under the house. Though his father had put up a swing in the cellars he would not play there alone in the gloom. In his evocation of his childhood fears he contrasts the brightness and sunniness of innocence with a fatal logic and curiosity, a "meddling intellect", that

[35] *H.G.*, pp. 22-4. [36] *Op. cit.*, pp. 159-65.
[37] See Webster, *op. cit.*, p. 16.

brought the shadow of darkness to contaminate his happiness. This contrast between innocence and experience, and their incompatibility expressed in terms of light and dark recur as powerful metaphors in his writing, notably in *Lord of the Flies*, *Pincher Martin*, and *Free Fall*. Part of the unease communicated by Golding's work which disturbs and fascinates his readers is, in fact, first generated in himself:

> One afternoon I was sitting on the wall that divided our garden from the churchyard. Eight, was I, perhaps or nine? Or older even? There is nothing by which I can tell. I contemplated the stones a few feet away and saw suddenly that several of them were flat up against our wall. I remember knowing then that I had seen and thought enough. My nights were miserable as it was, with every sort of apprehension given a label, and these even so only outliers of a central, not-comprehended dark. But the sun shone on the wall and I watched the inside of my head go on and take step after logical step. At which end of a grave does a stone stand? I remembered the sexton, Mr Baker, calling them headstones and I made the final deduction that the dead lay, their heads under our wall, the rest of them projecting from their own place into our garden, their feet, their knees even, tucked under our lawn.
>
> Logic is insistent. I recall an awareness at that moment that I was being foolish; that the demonstration of this proposition would do no one any good and me a great deal of harm. The lawn, almost the only uncontaminated place in that ancient neighbourhood, had been sunny and innocent until my deliberate exercise of logic had invited the enemy in.
>
> What was that enemy? I cannot tell. He came with darkness. . . . In daylight I thought of the Roman remains that had been dug up under the church as the oldest things near, sane things from sane people

like myself. But at night, the Norman door and pillar, even the flint wall of our cellar, were older, far older, were rooted in the darkness under the earth.[38]

The world of stability and sanity is represented by the portrait of his father who appeared to Golding as "incarnate omniscience", capable of doing anything he wished from wood-carving to painting, from geography and natural history to playing several musical instruments and making his own crystal set. From this admirable world of security the boy's escape was to sit alone up the chestnut tree in the garden in a private world where he could read and imagine as he liked, a world, too, from which he could look out on passers-by. Eventually private irrational fears had to be squared with practical existence and, contrary to his real feelings, he allowed himself to be persuaded to take up a scientific career, more or less to please his parents. But what his father stood for was the idea of a perfectible society and Golding was later to find this clashing with his own experience:

. . . my career was to be a scientific one. Science was busy clearing up the universe. There was no place in this exquisitely logical universe for the terrors of darkness . . . even in daylight now, the dead under the wall drew up the green coverlet of our grass and lay back with a heart-squeezing grin . . . though the march of science was irresistible, its path did not lie through my particular darkness.[39]

There were to be misgivings and finally an acceptance of the fact that life has to be grasped with all that is dark and inexplicable in human nature. The rational alone has no monopoly:

I was glad about science in a remote sort of way. If you were going to be anything, then a scientist was

[38] *H.G.*, p. 167. [39] *Op. cit.*, pp. 172-3.

what you ought to be. But the ladder was so long. In this dreary mood of personal knowledge and prophecy I knew that I should climb it; knew too that the darkness was all around, inexplicable, unexorcised, haunted, a gulf across which the ladder lay without reaching to the light.[40]

It could easily appear from Golding's background, and ideas, that his personality exists by a process of reaction against Victorian and Edwardian ideals of comfortable progress ever spiralling onward until shattered by the First World War. This would be to make of him a gloomy, belly-aching writer with no constructive values to offer, simply describing the ruins that lie about us. In fact, his great virtue as a writer, in spite of the sombre quality of his work, is precisely to underline the need for self-awareness, the need to look evil in the face and root out self-deception—all being themes he fully realises as fiction so as to make them, even if unpleasant, unforgettable. Nor can anyone ignore his great technical gifts and his tenacity of purpose. *The Inheritors* was written in twenty-eight days in spare time during teaching in all the bustle of a school staff-room; *Pincher Martin* was drafted in sixteen days. Golding seems untroubled by life around him as he writes and is able to make his own interior solitude. He takes two or three years to think over a work first, but then writes quickly.[41] There is an obvious advantage in this method for the concentration and careful shaping of his books. It certainly succeeds in *The Inheritors* and *Pincher Martin*, where the overall unity recalls the dynamic force of great poetry. When all the argument over Golding as a moralist or a prophet is laid aside it will be for his perceptiveness as a poet and his genius for making the reader re-experience basic feelings and urges that he will be

[40] *Op. cit.*, p. 174.
[41] See Davis, *op. cit.*, p. 29; Webster, *op. cit.*, p. 16.

esteemed. It is characteristic of him that he envisages his purpose not as that of a preacher but as that of a creative artist:

> In all the books I have suggested a shape in the universe that may, as it were, account for things. The greatest pleasure is not—say—sex or geometry. It is just understanding. And if you can get people to understand their own humanity—well, that's the job of the writer.[42]

[42] Webster, *op. cit.*, p. 16.

CHAPTER II

THE METAPHOR OF DARKNESS: *LORD OF THE FLIES*

Making people understand their own humanity, which Golding sees as the basic quality in a writer, can be narrowed down to mean, in his case, making people become self-aware and honest with themselves about the condition they find themselves in, and the kind of life they lead. The characters he creates and the presentation of their behaviour and motives are aids to the understanding of the darkness that lies in the heart of man. For Golding the dark places are very real, as "The Ladder and the Tree" shows, and all his work seems to be a coming-to-terms with them. He is determined they shall be understood; salvation and sanity seem to lie in the complete and honest understanding of the evil that resides in us.

The novels not only demonstrate this but also convey Golding's urgent feeling about his point of view. The boys isolated on the island in *Lord of the Flies* discover their true natures but also illustrate both the depravity and the nobility in human nature. The new men in *The Inheritors* show unflatteringly how the human race must make its way. Pincher Martin is tortured until he comes to the full realisation of the wickedness of his past. Sammy in *Free Fall* sets out explicitly in search of his true self but what he uncovers is mainly unpleasant. Father Jocelin in *The Spire*, in delirium on his deathbed, recognises his foul spiritual pride and all the shady sexual motives hidden behind his vision of being architect for God's glory. The total effect is not gloom but a serenity of understanding that looks at the human condition frankly and admits and resolves the contradictions we are all aware of and torn between: life is both a fine thing and a corrupt thing, both sunny and dark. Golding describes the presence of these two elements in his outlook on life in "The Ladder and the Tree", quoted above, together with the idea that a "meddling intellect" inevitably destroys innocence.

In the novels the idea of darkness becomes very complex in its terms of reference. It becomes particular faults of character, especially selfishness and greed. It becomes the urge to use other people, to exploit them, an urge none can escape, as with the new men triumphing over the apemen or Sammy using Beatrice Ifor. It becomes the urge to power and violence, notably with certain of the boys in *Lord of the Flies* where, in its crudest form, it is superstition and explains the setting-up of the pig's head on a stick. It can be blinding vanity as it is for Jocelin. More than anything it is the split between body and soul.

There is, in the novels, a steady progression from the first oblique statements about this split between body and soul to a more explicitly intellectual discussion of the problem. The ending of *The Spire* comes nearest to the resolution of it. To take the novels in sequence: the groups in *Lord of the Flies* and in *The Inheritors* act out a drama in which the reader is left to draw his own conclusions. In *Pincher Martin*, the drama of a single individual, the author is more explicit and leads us firmly to the interpretation he wants. We are taken down into the cellars of Pincher's mind—this is Golding's own image—and shown what he must face there: the knowledge that life is not appetite alone:

> Well of darkness. Down, pad, down. Coffin ends crushed in the wall. Under the churchyard back through the death door to meet the master.[1]

[1] *P.M.*, p. 178.

We are shown how Pincher is forced to admit what, in the imagined fullness of his life, he has been running away from.

The idea of avoiding the final answer, of spiritual cowardice, is applied also to Sammy Mountjoy in *Free Fall*. Where Pincher Martin found himself floundering in the sea and was obliged only *in extremis* to question his behaviour in life, Sammy on the other hand begins with apparent honesty and the best will in the world to analyse his existence from as far back as he can go. He seems to be an improvement on Pincher Martin in that he is not blind to his shortcomings and, in a sense, wants to atone for them. But when it comes to the crisis he balks the issue and runs away. After having examined his life he sees the way to join up body and soul. He sees his selfishness at the end of the novel in perspective but no bridge (the image Golding uses) between the physical and spiritual worlds.

Father Jocelin in *The Spire* goes one step further. Without the benefit of Sammy's analytical powers he is forced by circumstances to admit that all along his true motives have been mixed. He combines the elemental quality the author put into Pincher with the honest intentions of the analytical Sammy and reveals to us a creature who, in fever on his deathbed, sweats out the truth about himself and the position of man in the world. We are committed in various ways to consuming each other and there is no one to guide us. We are alone. For we see and understand everything in terms of our self-centred bodies. Jocelin sees through this trap but his revelation of the isolation of man is only a wisp of thought, unexpressed in formal terms, drifting through his mind:

> . . . he saw all people naked, creatures of light brown parchment, which bound in their pipes or struts. He saw them pace or prance in sheets of woven stuff, with

the skins of dead animals under their feet and he began to struggle and gasp to leave this vision behind him in words that never reached the air.

How proud their hope of hell is. There is no innocent work. God knows where God may be.[2]

When Jocelin dies the priest gives him absolution but he has already found his own absolution in his private thoughts, without need of any sacrament. He seems to be the fullest realisation of Golding's ideal of man who finally comes to terms with the "cellarage", the word Golding uses to describe what Jocelin, throughout his life, has been wearing his body out in avoiding. Golding implies that this is the furthest one can go in self-knowledge. But by bringing this self-knowledge to Jocelin on his death-bed he further implies that its practical application in the ordinary run of existence is too difficult.

In *Lord of the Flies* Golding immediately comes to terms in a masterly way with his main preoccupation: the problem of evil. He shows how evil is dormant in human nature and how the world may appear a sunny place when in fact the corruption of darkness can arise from man himself and cast shadows over it. We learn that the boys are sole survivors of an aircrash which occurs when they are being evacuated to the southern hemisphere during some future catastrophic war. The island they find themselves on could be a happy playground and, at the very beginning of the book, Ralph in sheer delight at being on a real coral island stands on his head and looks at Piggy through his legs. But this is only the point of departure that Golding's book shares with R. M. Ballantyne's *The Coral Island* (1858), the avowed original for his thoughts on the theme of innocence and experience. Thereafter the gap of divergence grows ever wider. His view of the Ballantyne situation he considers

[2] *T.S.*, p. 222.

to be ironic, not in the bad sense "but in almost a compassionate sense", and he goes on to explain:

> You see, really, I'm getting at myself in this. What I'm saying to myself is "don't be such a fool, you remember when you were a boy . . . you lived on that island with Ralph and Jack and Peterkin . . . Now you are grown up, you are adult; it's taken you a long time to become adult, but now you've got there you can see that people are not like that; they would not behave like that if they were God-fearing English gentlemen and they went to an island like that". Their savagery would not be found in natives on an island. As like as not they would find savages who were kindly and uncomplicated and that the devil would rise out of the intellectual complications of the three white men on the island itself.[3]

He objects to *Lord of the Flies* being thought of as a black mass version of Ballantyne and sees it as a realistic view of the situation.[4]

In Ballantyne's book Ralph Rover, Jack Martin, and Peterkin Gay are three "jolly young tars" for whom being shipwrecked is so jolly for the world is kind. Ralph, the narrator, frequently refers to "the great and kind Creator of this beautiful world". They are all considerate towards one another and exist in harmony: "There was indeed no note of discord whatever in the symphony we played together on that sweet Coral Island . . . (we were) tuned to the same key, namely that of Love! Yes, we loved one another with much fervency." There is no sense of irony; a severe storm does not cause any feeling of insecurity. They return home under a clear sky to find their cat cosily sleeping and waiting for them. Violence exists on Ballantyne's Coral Island but it comes from outside with the arrival of the cannibals and the pirates

[3] F. Kermode, Interview with Golding for BBC, 28 Aug. 1959. See also *H.G.* pp. 88-9.
[4] BBC Interview.

(who kill the cat). The problem of evil is touched on. Ralph recognises "the strange mixture of good and evil that exists not only in the material earth but in our own natures". However, the effects of storms and the experience of the cannibals lead him to reflect that "the works of God are wonderful and His ways past finding out". All fits into a frame of benevolent planning. The latter part of Ballantyne's story, especially the conversion of the savages to Christianity, ends happily with the boys bound for home "leaving far behind us the beautiful bright green coral islands of the Pacific Ocean". The impression the reader is left with is that it was all very curious and interesting, even the self-slaughtering cannibals, and also a very edifying and jolly adventure.

In Golding's story the possibility of discord soon makes its appearance. A group has already gathered around Ralph in an attempt to establish an assembly, with their newly found conch as symbol of order, when Jack and the choir come trudging over the beach. The beginnings of the degeneration of his society lie in Jack's natural arrogance:

> The boy (Jack) came close and peered down at Ralph, screwing up his face as he did so. What he saw of the fair-haired boy with the creamy shell on his knees did not seem to satisfy him . . .
>
> "I ought to be chief", said Jack with simple arrogance, "because I'm chapter chorister and head boy. I can sing C sharp."[5]

They do not really trust each other. Jack is given second place as chief of the hunting choir, but it is not long before the rankling of this failure causes a split and leads to Jack being chief on his own terms. The position then becomes Ralph, Piggy, and Simon versus Jack and the choir-hunters. Among the boys divided into the good and decent (Ralph-Piggy) and those who succumb to

[5] *L.F.*, pp. 27-9.

evil (Jack and his followers) Golding has placed a particular creation of his own: the visionary Simon.[6]

He is the prototype of Golding's ideal of man given fuller realisation in Jocelin in *The Spire*. The man Golding admires is the one who will look darkness in the face and, with great human courage, come to terms with the ignoble within us which is potentially destructive of our humanity. Simon, a quiet, withdrawn, skinny boy with a tendency to epilepsy, likes to wander off on his own in order to be alone. His usual haunt is a carefully enclosed glade. It is one of the ironies of the book that this "holy" place is the very spot where Jack and his hunters bring the head of the pig, impale it, and revere it. This pig's head, rotting on its stick, is the Lord of the Flies, Beelzebub, Evil, the Dark. Simon looks at it hard. He is seeing the symbol of the evil Golding describes as being in us. It is only the outward form of those forces that work in Jack and the hunters turning them into murderers. The pig's head is described as a "Gift for the Darkness", but a gift cannot drive the darkness away and hunting the Beast and killing it are an illusion. The evil is inside people and ineradicable. As Simon looks at the pig's head he learns this:

> "Fancy thinking the Beast was something you could hunt and kill!" said the head. For a moment or two the forest and all the other dimly appreciated places echoed with the parody of laughter. "You knew, didn't you? I'm part of you? Close, close, close! I'm the reason why it's no go? Why things are what they are?" . . . Simon's head wobbled. His eyes were half-closed as though he were imitating the obscene thing on the stick. He knew that one of his times was coming on. The Lord of the Flies was expanding like a balloon . . .
>
> Simon found he was looking into a vast mouth.

[6] Suggested by Peterkin in Ballantyne, *i.e.* "Simon called Peter" as Golding explains in BBC Interview.

> There was blackness within, a blackness that spread . . .
> Simon was inside the mouth. He fell down and lost consciousness.[7]

This moment, in the heart of the book, shows Golding's art at its finest. The incident and Simon's fit are described on a naturalistic level but at the same time the reader is aware of the author's symbolic intention working through—an intention all the richer in its force for its obliqueness. When Simon imagines he has fainted into the mouth of the Beast the author is getting over his point that the pig's head is only an external device for referring to the evil that is within people. Simon's awareness of it is not of something outside himself but a recognition that it is potentially within all people whether they are good or bad, hence the associating of it with himself physically, his acceptance of it, as he faints into the Beast's jaws.

The characters, in fact, are not conveniently divided up into "goodies" and "baddies", though Jack and Simon do lie towards the extremes. Both Ralph for all his decency and Piggy for all his commonsense are involved in murder, and both are willing to accept the meat of the hunters in spite of their principles. It is the complexity of human nature that accommodates the possibilities of both good and evil and this is reflected in Simon's own private thoughts on the nature of the Beast:

> However Simon thought of the Beast, there rose before his inward sight the picture of a human at once heroic and sick.[8]

Night time on the island and the children's night fears have prompted irrational feelings and silly talk of a monster. But this is only a side-issue compared with the real evil developing in some members of the group. It is given to Simon, wandering perplexed after his inter-

[7] *L.F.*, pp. 177-8. [8] *Op. cit.*, p. 128.

view with the pig's head, to discover the real cause for the talk of a supernatural monster inhabiting the island. It is he who discovers that the cause of their fears is the pathetic rotting corpse of a parachutist that has drifted down from an overhead battle. He looks with noble compassion on this figure caught among the rocks:

> The tangle of lines showed him the mechanics of this parody; he examined the white nasal bones, the teeth, the colours of corruption. He saw how pitilessly the layers of rubber and canvas held together the poor body that should be rotting away. Then the wind blew again and the figure lifted, bowed, and breathed foully at him. Simon knelt on all fours and was sick till his stomach was empty. Then he took the lines in his hands; he freed them from the rocks and the figure from the wind's indignity.[9]

Having faced Evil he can face the Dark and has, in doing so, discovered the truth—both the literal truth that the monster does not exist and the deeper truth that the boys have nothing to fear but themselves. But for Golding's ideal of man, the full knowledge of life, of the truth, cannot survive in the full reality of ordinary existence. Pincher Martin and Sammy Mountjoy are brought to the verge of self-knowledge and no further. Those who cross the boundary must die, as Simon must and Jocelin must. It is Simon's tragic fate, and another irony of the book, that this bringer of enlightening news is killed in the frenzied dance in praise of the hunt, in praise of the Beast, conducted by Jack and all the boys on the shore. Unlike Father Jocelin Simon is innocent, preserving still that innocence that Sammy in *Free Fall* goes in search of. The particular quality of Simon is to be "a lover of mankind, a visionary, who reaches commonsense attitudes not by reason but by intuition" and to be "a Christ-figure in my fable" as Golding himself

[9] *Op. cit.*, p. 181.

states.[10] He calls Simon a saint and sees him going away to his glade like the child Vianney, the future Curé d'Ars. Any difficulty in understanding Simon exists only for the sophisticated; the illiterate find it easy to understand Simon voluntarily embracing the Beast, giving the news to "the ordinary bestial man on the beach" and being killed for it.[11] It is for this reason that the removal of Simon's body by the tide is described in terms that are magical and naturalistic at the same time, so that he is naturally and not at all picturesquely re-absorbed and embraced by the material world. This recalls how his own quality of intuitive understanding had been one of all-embracing completeness:

> The water rose further and dressed Simon's coarse hair with brightness. The line of his cheek silvered and the turn of his shoulder became sculptured marble. The strange, attendant creatures, with their fiery eyes and trailing vapours, busied themselves round his head. The body lifted a fraction of an inch from the sand and a bubble of air escaped from the mouth with a wet plop. Then it turned gently in the water.
>
> Somewhere over the darkened curve of the world the sun and moon were pulling; and the film of water on the earth planet was held, bulging slightly on one side while the solid core turned. The great wave of the tide moved further along the island and the water lifted. Softly, surrounded by a fringe of inquisitive bright creatures, itself a silver shape beneath the steadfast constellations, Simon's dead body moved out towards the open sea.[12]

There is more violence: a littlun killed by accident in a fire on the Island, the obscene hunting of Ralph, and the killing of Piggy. To read the description of the death

[10] See "Fable" in *H.G.*, pp. 97-8.
[11] BBC Interview.
[12] *L.F.*, p. 190.

of Piggy immediately after that of Simon is very revealing for the interpretation the reader feels obliged, through the stylistic devices, to place on the book. Piggy, holding the conch in his hands, is struck a glancing blow from a deliberately aimed boulder, and he and the symbol of order are shattered. He falls onto a platform of rock in the sea and the waves simply wash the body away. The description is brief, matter-of-fact; Piggy is a piece of flotsam and the sea does not dignify his departure as it does Simon's.[13] Golding manages to deepen his meaning of what the boys' attitudes represent by providing them, in their common ends, with descriptions that correspond to the limited practical intelligence in the case of Piggy—dry in tone—and the intuitive depth of understanding in the case of Simon—eloquent and transfiguring. It is obvious that Golding favours, and would wish the reader to favour, the rarer qualities of Simon, described by one commentator as "the one character that the book clearly endorses" and whose qualities are "those that the novel itself expresses and promotes in its readers".[14]

On the other hand another commentator has attempted to outline a case against Simon even to the extent of making the unwarranted assumption that the author should have cut him out in an early draft.[15] The objection is based on a misunderstanding of the text. It seems that we should not accept Simon bringing the news about the dead airman because his discovery that the Beast is rationally explicable would invalidate his symbolic value and would be out of character in a mystic. This ignores the fact that Simon's message is twofold since in bringing the boys news that the Beast does not exist outside them

[13] *L.F.*, pp. 222-3.

[14] Philippa Moody, *A Critical Commentary on L.F.*, London 1966, p. 30.

[15] H. H. Taylor, "The Case against William Golding's Simon-Piggy", *Contemporary Review*, Sep. 1966.

he is also bearing witness to the grimmer truth that it exists within. The real hero, according to this view, is Piggy who reaches the same conclusion as Simon that there is nothing to fear unless it is other people, and he loses his life in facing up to Jack. Simon on this score then becomes a pretentious enrichment of the symbolism of the book and the irony that Piggy is honourable but limited is lost.

This kind of approach which tends not to allow the text to speak for itself is typical of some of the considerable criticism *Lord of the Flies* has received in its short career. Some commentators have felt obliged to label the characters with points of view that they are alleged to stand for and thereafter unwittingly falsify Golding's fictional creation to fit into their favoured thesis—that he is a pessimist, maybe, or an optimist or a Freudian. This has happened particularly in the case of this novel and has not been left without comment by the author.

It is tempting, for instance, to cast the boys in roles that correspond to different facets of personality in the Freudian manner, so that one is *ego* another *id* and so on. This kind of approach has been fully put by Claire Rosenfield for whom Ralph is God, Jack the Devil, Piggy a father-figure, Simon a victim in primitive sacrifice, and Piggy again, in his death, a case of symbolic cannibalism.[16] Almost any illustration from Freud, particularly from his *Totem and Taboo*, can be made plausible by picking out of *Lord of The Flies* those elements that suit the thesis. Very soon the author's own voice is drowned. Thus Claire Rosenfield can categorically claim that "events have simply supported Freud's conclusions that no child is innocent": but this ignores the central position given to Simon and to the author's attempts to assert that he was the exception among the boys. She also claims that in Golding's view bestiality

[16] Claire Rosenfield, "Men of Smaller Growth. A Psychological Analysis of *L.F.*", *Literature and Psychology*, Autumn 1961.

and irrationality dominate "all men, even the most rational and civilised". But again Simon, Golding's unique creation, does not fit here. When she does attempt to fit Simon into the Freudian view she is forced to simplify and so falsify. For her, Simon at his death "becomes not a substitute for beast, but beast itself". Golding has, in another connexion, explained this quite simply: Simon during the dance "*doesn't* become the beast, he becomes the beast *in other people's opinions*".[17] She is too hasty in claiming that Golding is consciously dramatising Freudian theory and a similar position taken by William Wasserstrom who sees Ralph as *ego*, Piggy as *super-ego*, and Jack as *id* is equally unhelpful.[18] Golding, even allowing for exaggeration, denies this approach quite flatly:

> And to think I've never read Freud in my life. Someone wrote a terribly erudite article showing that Ralph was an *id* and Piggy an *ego*. Or was it the other way round? I was quite impressed, but the whole thing was simply untrue. I suppose I'm doing the same thing as Freud did—investigating this complex phenomenon called man. Perhaps our results are similar, but there is no influence.[19]

There has been, on the other hand, a tendency towards a political interpretation with the roles redistributed. Ralph is "*l'homme moyen sensuel* but even more clearly the 'liberal' politician who has found he can talk fluently and enjoys the applause of the crowd".[20] In this way Piggy's commonsense and his position as outsider

[17] BBC Interview.

[18] W. Wasserstrom, "Reason and Reverence in Art and Science", *Literature and Psychology*, Winter 1962. See also comments by E. L. Epstein to Capricorn Paperback ed. of *L.F.*, 1959 for more Freudian interpretations.

[19] B. Dick, "The Novelist is a Displaced Person. An Interview with Golding", *College English*, Mar. 1965, p. 481.

[20] K. Watson, "A Reading of *L.F.*", *English*, Spring 1964, p. 4.

among the other middle-class boys underline social attitudes so that he appears as a democrat and intellecttual in opposition to the "officer class", with its automatic assumption of leadership. Samneric represent the nonentities of good will most of us became when faced with crises and Jack, with Roger, his henchman, like a potential concentration camp guard, becomes a Hitler. But once again the character who cannot be fully fitted into this scheme of things is Simon who simply cannot be described as representing integrity. And if the political fable should have such importance one might well ask why absolute power corrupts only Jack when Ralph is just as vulnerable in his position of authority.

The force of the book is such that behind these views is the assumption of a meaning in actuality far more important than the fiction itself, a feeling that there is a message to decipher and once deciphered the book can be ignored.[21] The main difficulty with *Lord of the Flies* has been, from the outset, deciding its form; a similar problem arises for the other novels. Sure enough there is meaning in it beyond the fiction itself; there is allegory in it somewhere but the reader should not forget that the themes and characters first emerged into his consciousness as part of a work of imagination and that to discuss them out of that context is only a convention it would be wrong to forget.

Whatever label is finally decided on it is certainly a work that presents a challenge to the reader who at the end must question his attitudes to the book; to pass over it as an entertainment is impossible. There is the feeling that if it is an allegory then what is the author trying to convince us of? Though to some the allegory is sombre

[21] For hostile criticism of the kind where dislike of the "message" leads to denigration of the work see particularly, M. Green: "Distaste for the Contemporary", *The Nation*, 21 May 1960; J. M. Egan, "Golding's view of Man", *America*, 26 Jan. 1963; L. J. Halle, "Small Savages", *Saturday Review*, 15 Oct. 1955.

but realistic to others it appears as a falsely black and impossible view of man. This alleged negative meaning of the work has occasioned some of the unwillingness to admit its literary worth.

One of the main disputes has centred round the question, should one go for Golding or Salinger, *Lord of the Flies* or *The Catcher in the Rye*? This has been particularly an American interest because of the rivalry and popularity of these two works among American students. There is also an element of the modish in it but more generally what is at stake is the opposition between the pictures of youth and society that these two works give—Salinger's with his Holden Caulfield, innocent until corrupted by society which is phoney through and through, and Golding's with his boys potentially evil at the outset. The dispute depends upon oversimplifying and omitting subtleties. As we have seen, Golding's emphasis is on potential evil and, for his elect like Simon, even the absence of evil. His picture, in fact, is realistic since even the decent Ralph likes to hunt and but for his respect for the rules which he says are "all we've got" could be a hunter too. It is details of this kind which give the book its fine quality as a composition that have got lost in the argument over whether Golding is presenting us with an optimistic or a pessimistic view of life. F. E. Kearns has placed *The Catcher in the Rye* in the tradition of the innate goodness of man until corrupted by society and *Lord of the Flies* in the tradition of the insuperable depravity of human nature which makes all human effort at justice or order futile, hoping to prove that Golding's book is one of unrelieved pessimism.[22] He stresses that even if Ralph is saved he is saved, in the person of the naval officer, by a sophisticated form of the violence he is running from. Ralph must return to a world at war, which in turn shows that whatever free will exists it is

[22] F. E. Kearns, "Salinger and Golding; Conflict on the Campus", *America*, 26 Jan. 1963.

doomed to be ineffectual.[23] He is able to quote Golding's own comment on the saving of Ralph: "And who will rescue the adult and his cruiser?"[24] but misses the irony of the ending. This effectively transfers the action from the island back to life at large but also makes the reader automatically apply the story he has read to adult life where its obliquely stated truths are meant to have their full impact. F. E. Kearns does not see that Golding is not, in underlining the inevitability of evil, approving it. What he approves is the contrary of evil, but shut his eyes to the existence of evil he will not, as his Simon does not. In his determination to be human and tolerant and not succumb to evil or man's dark side Golding is compassionate and realistic. Man's nobility is to stare the Beast in the face rather than pretend it does not exist. Ralph weeps "for the end of innocence, the darkness of man's heart, and the fall through the air of the true, wise friend called Piggy". He has travelled a long sobering journey from the moment of high spirits when he stood on his head. He does not weep for Simon or even know, as the reader does, of his vision of their life. The "saint" has been completely ineffectual, to Ralph, from the practical point of view: but he is not meant to be for the reader who returns with Ralph, to our normal world of dissensions and war. The message, if it has to be insisted upon, does not fit easily into the categories: pessimistic or optimistic. It is not that man is either good or evil but simply that he is capable of becoming, and needs to become, self-aware. Golding is stating our problems, reminding us of them or even making us re-experience them, but it is too much to expect him to solve them. Criticism which goes straight for the message presupposes that the author is offering solutions when

[23] F. E. Kearns & L. M. Grande, "An exchange of views: 'The Appeal of Golding' ", *Commonweal*, 22 Feb. 1963.

[24] F. E. Kearns, "Golding revisited" in *William Golding's L.F. A Source Book*, ed. William Nelson, New York 1963, pp. 165-9.

in fact he is only offering an imaginative experience.

The return to normality at the end of *Lord of the Flies* where, because of the power of the book and especially of the description of the hunt, every reader expects Ralph to be annihilated constitutes the celebrated "gimmick" ending. The term is Golding's own,[25] but it has unfortunately been taken up without the qualifications he appended to it and, instead of meaning a legitimate contrivance, has been interpreted mostly in the sense of a trick or even a let-down. He has explained that in *Lord of the Flies*, *The Inheritors*, and *Pincher Martin* it was essential as an aid to putting over what he wanted to say:

> . . . I have a view which you haven't got and I would like you to see this from my point of view. Therefore, I must first put it so graphically in my way of thinking that you identify yourself with it, and then at the end I'm going to put you where you are, looking at it from outside.[26]

Each case of this deliberate change of viewpoint must be taken on its merits but in *Lord of the Flies*, at least, it is difficult to agree with James Gindin who has objected to the use of the gimmick because it "palliates the force and the unity of the original metaphor".[27] When he writes: "If the adult world rescues the boys are the depravity and brutality of human nature so complete?" he is simply forgetting the irony of a rescuer who is also a hunter but doesn't know it.[28]

Golding expects his reader to be very careful; it is strange therefore that he has so often been accused both of being too explicit and too obscure. He is clearly committed to writing in such a style that he can entrap the reader into seeing everything his way and only at the end allow him to escape so that he can reconsider it from

[25] BBC Interview. [26] *Ibid.*

[27] James Gindin, *Post-War British Fiction*, London 1962, p. 204.

[28] See Dick, *op. cit.*, p. 481. Golding's own comment.

his own point of view, outside the tale. This explains the extremely close direction of events so that compared with most novels action and character-development seem to lack the free give and take of ordinary life. This special conditioning is a mark of all Golding's work and where it has been thought that the moral intentions have become too obvious some readers have felt that the freedom of the novel-form has been sacrificed to allegorical statements. Some of the first comments on *Lord of the Flies* made much of this while conceding its excellent quality and the author's great skill. Walter Allen found that the burden on the children was "too unnaturally heavy for it to be possible to draw conclusions" from the book.[29] Douglas Hewitt, however, saw the weaknesses in the tendency to be too explicit; the pig's head scene in particular was too pat to be plausible.[30] Margaret Walters, likewise, attacks the stress placed on Simon as being obtrusive and obvious though on the whole she considers Golding succeeds in uniting idea, character, and situation, particularly by his ironic references throughout to the world of adults.[31] The main charge, however, is clearly that Golding has omitted—in a way unbecoming in a novelist—the complexities of ordinary life.[32]

Such objections seem inevitable to any kind of allegorical fiction. But how far can they be taken in this case? The author himself accepts the term fable to describe *Lord of the Flies* but is fully aware that the novelist ought not to preach overtly.[33] He has also distinguished "myth" and "fable" bringing out the deliberate contrivance necessary to the latter:

[29] W. Allen, "New Novels", *New Statesman*, 25 Sep. 1954.
[30] D. Hewitt, "New Novels", *Manchester Guardian*, 28 Sep. 1954.
[31] M. Walters, "Two fabulists: Golding and Camus", *Melbourne Critical Review*, vol. 4, 1961.
[32] J. Peter, "Fables of William Golding", *Kenyon Review*, Fall 1957, p. 584.
[33] *H.G.*, p. 94.

> . . . what I would regard as a tremendous compliment to myself would be if someone would substitute the word "myth" for "fable" because I think a myth is a much profounder and more significant thing than a fable. I do feel fable as being an invented thing on the surface whereas myth is something which comes out from the roots of things in the ancient sense of being the key to existence, the whole meaning of life, and experience as a whole.[34]

Legitimate contrivance is necessary to any kind of fiction and instances of contrivance must be measured against the imaginative force of their context before being condemned. No sensible critic of *Lord of the Flies* has ever denied its great brilliance and power and yet it has been summed up by Walter Allen as "a considerable confidence-trick". His view tends to take the fable too literally:

> . . . the behaviour of the children is taken, as many of Golding's admirers seem to take it, as paradigmatic of general human behaviour in the absence of restraint. There can be no conceivable parallel at all, as would be plain if Golding had lowered the age-range of his boys from roughly five years old to twelve to, say, from one to seven.[35]

Objections of this kind can easily prompt others equally irrelevant: such as, why are there no girls? why no talk of sex? etc. But the fabulist deliberately contrives to concentrate his story and his characters so that they have the force of images which create, if successful, the inescapable feeling, not that what happens is plausible, so much as convincing in its essence. This is the poetic quality of Golding's fiction, successful in *Lord of the Flies* by its overwhelming sense of the potential evil and

[34] BBC Interview.

[35] W. Allen, *Tradition and Dream*, Pelican edn., Harmondsworth 1965, p. 310.

potential good in man, suggested basically by the image of child as potential adult.

His novel is sufficiently naturalistic for his purpose and has been described as "naturalistic-allegorical".[36] Though to hunt pedantically for symbols and parallels would be to destroy pleasure in the book, nevertheless any reader comes upon the rich texture with delight in its interlocking design where every incident or description upon reflexion illuminates something else. There is a particular pleasure in the sense of nothing wasted.[37] It's the literary approach that yields most from the text without forcing. In broad outline there is a progression from innocence and fun to the sobering effect of grim experience, conveyed by the images of Ralph playful at the beginning and hard-pressed and weeping at the end. Other images interlock: his discovery of the island grows less lovely as things deteriorate; the odour of decay pervades life from the diarrhoea of the littluns happily eating the fruit to Jack hunting the pigs by following their steaming droppings; the association of the Beast, evil, excrement, and blood is both overpowering and purposeful. There is in general a progression from light to dark.

Lord of the Flies was a triumph for Golding but also a test-case. He has survived principally through the poetic conviction of his composition. Critical attitudes and ideas arise when the book is finished; during the reading one is eager to know what happened next, to feel what nerve will be unerringly touched on next rather than to assess what all these complexities add up to. Because of the moralistic intention in his work Golding has been too easily pushed into the role of explainer when he is only being what one expects the novelist to be—a describer.

[36] B. S. Oldsey and S. Weintraub: *The Art of William Golding*, New York 1965, p. 33.

[37] See M. Kinkead-Weekes and I. Gregor, *William Golding. A Critical Study*, London 1967, pp. 15-64 for a sensitive and appreciative commentary.

CHAPTER III

INNOCENCE AND KNOWLEDGE: *THE INHERITORS*

The poetic richness and suggestiveness of *The Inheritors* has called forth both great praise and sharp condemnation. Certainly, Golding takes great risks with his second novel—risks of obscurity in the first and last chapters, and loss of the reader's interest until nearly half way through the book because of the absence of incident. He overcomes these and the reader is rewarded for getting used to the strangeness of presentation—admittedly not an easy thing. Of all the novels Golding considers it his favourite and his best.[1]

It is the clearest illustration of Golding's belief that a novelist should, on the technical side, not merely repeat himself. *Lord of the Flies* is perhaps the only one of his novels to allow an easy approach. With *The Inheritors* he simply sacrifices all that would make the book too immediately accessible: there is little narrative; there is no detail that is not significant, though no reader can hope to get them all on a first reading; above all, the choice of setting would seem at first glance quite intractable, being the decline and fall of the immediate predecessors of *homo sapiens*.

Both for his point of view on the human condition and for the angle of presentation Golding is indebted to H. G. Wells, but indebted in the sense that he takes his strength from inverting the type of attitude Wells advocates in his *Outline of History*, in the chapters on Neander-

[1] See B. Dick, "The Novelist is a Displaced Person. An interview with Golding", *College English*, Mar. 1965, p. 481.

thal man, and attempts to illustrate in narrative terms in his story called *The Grisly Folk.* It was the excessively optimistic tone of Wells that prompted Golding's reaction. Wells writes of "the coming of men like ourselves" as an "enormous leap forward in the history of mankind". Golding explains:

> Wells' *Outline of History* played a great part in my life because my father was a rationalist, and the *Outline of History* was something he took neat. Well now, Wells' *Outline of History* is the rationalist gospel *in excelsis* I should think. I got this from my father, and by and by it seemed to me not to be large enough. It seemed to me to be too neat and too slick. And when I re-read it as an adult I came across his picture of Neanderthal man, our immediate predecessors, as being these gross brutal creatures who were possibly the basis of the mythological bad man, whatever he may be, the ogre. I thought to myself that this is just absurd. What we're doing is externalising our own inside.[2]

It is not only the rather complacent tone but also the attitude of superiority on Wells' part that explains the quotation from the *Outline of History* placed at the head of *The Inheritors.* To be fair to Wells it should be pointed out that the stressing of the ugliness of the Neanderthalers in the quotation, and so his acceptance of Sir Harry Johnston's view that they may survive in racial memory as ogres, is his attempt to explain why there was no interbreeding between Neanderthalers and the Palaeolithic races. Indeed, it would have helped Golding's readers if this reference had not been cut since it reveals the feeling of distaste Wells has for these inferior creatures and their lack of comeliness. It would have made the starting point for Golding's ironic reversal of the idea clearer.

[2] See F. Kermode, Interview with Golding for BBC, 28 Aug. 1959.

On the question of the angle of presentation there seems no doubt that Golding must have had Wells' short-story, *The Grisly Folk*, at the back of his mind and been prompted by a remark in it concerning the Neanderthalers to take up the very opposite imaginative viewpoint from Wells. Where Wells writes: "But the grisly folk we cannot begin to understand. We cannot conceive in our different minds the strange ideas that chased one another through those queerly shaped brains. As well might we try to dream and feel as a gorilla dreams and feels", Golding in fact attempts to do just that. He sets before us the final days in the life of a small group of Neanderthalers whom he calls "the people": Lok and Fa, his mate; Ha and his mate, Nil with a babe-in-arms, "the new one"; the little girl Liku, the nameless Old Woman and Mal, the senior male of the group. Events are described almost entirely through the consciousness of this practically pre-verbal people.

Wells' short-story reads more like an essay than a tale and the elements of narrative in it are used as illustrations of the kind of life our ancestors lived in the struggle for survival against the marauding grisly folk. Wells imagines the fortunes of a wandering tribe from whom a girl is snatched and killed. He implies that it was in righteous self-defence that the true men, "these early pilgrim fathers of mankind", finally annihilated the grisly folk. Wells has no sympathy for the sub-human and nothing but admiration for our ancestors: "the strain of the victors was our strain; we are lineally identical with those sunbrown painted beings who ran and fought and helped one another." He cannot help suggesting the great victory it was for mankind; Golding's novel is written to show what a qualified victory we have behind us. He does not take the simple alternative, as some commentators have suggested, of showing Lok and "the people" as being better than the new men they encounter. His final position is one of objective observation on the very mixed future facing the new men as they journey to some new dwelling place.

In plot *The Inheritors* has at its core an incident in *The Grisly Folk*. Golding, however, has inverted it and imagines the snatching of the child as being the act of the new people who carry off the girl, Liku, and "the new one". We are meant to understand that aggression originates in the new people, the ones with whom we are "lineally identical", to use Wells' phrase. Golding goes to great length—five chapters—to show us first of all, and to make us re-experience, the life of the ape-men. In this group, at least, there are no tensions; all is shared—food, sex, responsibility, leadership, even sensory experience:

> One of the deep silences fell on them, that seemed so much more natural than speech, a timeless silence in which there were at first many minds in the overhang; and then perhaps no mind at all. So fully discounted was the roar of the water that the soft touch of the wind on the rocks became audible. Their ears as if endowed with separate life sorted the tangle of tiny sounds and accepted them, the sound of breathing, the sound of wet clay flaking and ashes falling in.[3]

Their relationship to the world is a passive and not an assertive one; they are children of earth, of Oa. This is their designation for the life force in Nature which they venerate in an objective and unsentimental way as provider and destroyer. To die is only to return to Oa's belly. The symbol of Oa is a root roughly figured like a gravid woman that Liku plays with as a doll: but, as a force, she is worshipped in natural forms as the ice-women.[4] "The people's" essential quality of meekness and innocence is suggested by this matriarchal veneration and also by the careful balance of duties between

[3] *T.I.*, p. 34.

[4] *Cf.* M. Kinkead-Weekes and I. Gregor, *William Golding. A Critical Study*, London 1967, p. 78.

the sexes: leadership is the province of men but women are particularly vessels of Oa. Lok feels his mate Fa to be at certain times removed from him by this quality of awe, as is the Old Woman, guardian of their fire. The Old Woman, in particular, is surrounded, for Lok, by an awesome quality that places her in a special category though we learn that she is also his most intimate link with Oa, his mother. There is a terrible moment for Lok when he finds the Old Woman's murdered body drifting in the river with water swilling in and out of her mouth "as though it had been nothing but a hole in a stone". The woman who was nearly Oa herself has become a mere thing and the reader feels this as the collapse of "the people's" way of seeing the world. Until then death, though bitter, had only been part of a process to be accepted with no feeling of the violation of what was natural; thus Mal, their leader, is buried with his knees drawn up to his chin in the warm earth by the fire with gifts of food and drink.

Part of the backcloth of this novel is in fact Lok's confusion about the place of Oa and the intuitive understanding of life he is used to in the new circumstances thrust upon him, circumstances which unlike what he has known demand action and male assertiveness. For nearly the whole of its length the book takes us into Lok's developing personality and transmits the feeling of a load placed on him greater than he can hope to bear or even understand.

The book begins in spring with the arrival of the apemen, led by Mal, at what are intended to be their summer quarters high above a waterfall. After the "dark winter cave by the sea" this suggests an emerging happiness, a paradise where the food is accessible and sweet, not bitter as they remember it by the sea. "The people's" first dilemma is to find a log to cross the swamp to their old haunts. The log they expected to find has gone. The reader will suspect it has been taken away but "the people" have no suspicions. In fact, linking up causal connexions of a direct kind, let alone hypotheses, is a long, hard process for them. Eventually they arrive at the idea of replacing the log by another and fitting it exactly as they need it. It is through their attitudes to this problem that Golding differentiates the members of the group. Mal remembers how it was done in the past when he was small and his position is one of authority. Of the males it is Ha who is more resourceful and begins to understand what Mal wants of him: but Lok is not so bright. He is, however, an attractive personality and full of fun. Crossing the log with Liku on his back is a great game and so too is looking for food. He is a charming character, always dreaming of nice things to eat; he is happy, carefree, playful; "thinking" is done by Mal and the Old Woman.

Connecting up evidence is particularly difficult for Lok. His senses catch faint suggestions of alien sounds, of smoke from another fire, but he cannot reason further. Ha, being more resourceful and curious, has perhaps reasoned further since he goes to look for wood and never returns. Lok investigates and finds not Ha but the scent of "the other". Mal, who had fallen in the water while crossing the log, dies of a chill, so leadership and responsibility fall on Lok. He continues his search for Ha and discovers the new people who appear to him as bone-faced. He is shot at but takes the twig-arrow as a present. He returns to Fa and finds all has been destroyed. Liku and the babe-in-arms have been snatched away and Nil and the Old Woman killed.

Where in *Lord of the Flies* Golding has been criticised for not being novelist enough with his character portrayal in *The Inheritors* he is not given his due in the subtler task of differentiating the child-like Lok and the intelligent Fa. It is she who takes the initiative in planning to take food to Liku and "the new one". Hidden in a tree, Lok and Fa observe the world of the new men, so full of contrasts with their own.[5] The point of view is Lok's and Fa's but the reader is aware that he is being privileged to share it; he knows he really belongs below in the clearing with the new people.[6] This device of allowing the reader to see himself from the outside unites the two main contrasting themes of the book. Where previously we were made aware of the passivity, harmony, and goodness of "the people", here we are shown the will-fulness, dissension, and disposition to evil of the new men. In them we are allowed to see in germ, via Lok and Fa, the qualities we consider truly human characteristics: drive, guile, control of their environment, the conflict of personality. Golding will also reveal but only at the end of the book, and from a completely different point of view, the new men's acquisition of the quality of self-awareness.

The world of the new men, since it is presented through the eyes of Lok and Fa, is shown for the most part by the contrasts it presents with their experience. The ape-men are mainly vegetarian and take meat only when they find it already killed by some wild animal, since then there is no "blame". The new men, on the other hand, are hunters and rely on superstitious ritual to help them, including a fetishistic stag-ceremony where a drawing is made on the ground and a man dresses as a stag. To make the hunt successful there is need for a mutilating sacrifice. This is the reverse of the ape-men's belief in Oa, source of life and death, with whom they are serenely one. This feeling of being integral with Nature, which is reflected in the harmony of their lives and the acceptance of a matriarchal outlook, contrasts with the masculine will-fulness of the new people whose emblem is a stag and

[5] *Cf.* "The Ladder and the Tree" in *H.G.*, p. 171 where the boy in the tree has glimpses of the unknown world of adult sexuality, innocent in this case.

[6] *Cf.* F. Kermode, "The Novels of William Golding", *International Literary Annual*, vol. iii, 1961, pp. 21-2.

where the balanced society of the ape-men is replaced by a patriarchal system of male domination and female subjection. Though the division of labour and role has given them greater flexibility as a social group, including the organisation of transport over water, they have lost, in spite of being human, that quality of tenderness and instinctive one-ness the ape-men still possess. This is best illustrated in their attitudes to sex. For Lok and Fa after their first escape from the new men, it is a source of comfort and unity in their fireless shelter: "The two pressed themselves against each other, they clung, searching for a centre, they fell, still clinging face to face. The fire of their bodies lit, and they strained towards it."[7] When Lok and Fa observe the new people at their drunken orgy they see two of them, Tuami and Vivani, in a violent and sadistic union in which they seem to have "consumed each other rather than lain together".

The biggest contrast between the ape-men and the new people is the latter's need to contain the violence and fear they have created in themselves. They cast the apemen in the role of devils and feel they must destroy them, if need be, with the aid of their superstition. Tuami's talent for drawing animals is put to grimmer use when he draws a grotesque and obscene picture of an ape-man on the wall of Lok's shelter and ties to it, with a stake hammered into the rock, a hostage to the devils—the girl Tanakil, who had "befriended" Liku. Where Wells writes in the *Outline of History*: "It greatly aids us to realise their common humanity that these earliest true men could draw", Golding has decided to suggest the questionable and confused feelings behind their accomplishment. This is the darkness of man's heart as superstition, and, in fact, the new men bring gifts of meat and fermented honey for the image of their devil; this is in contrast to the gifts of meat and drink for Mal in Oa's belly. Though each is in practical terms meaningless to

[7] *T.I.*, p. 131.

a modern reader they are tokens of fear on the one hand and serenity on the other.

There is a driving urge in Oa as well as serenity and it is this urge that provides the last stand of Lok and Fa. Lok, without knowing it, senses he must rescue Liku so that the race may continue. Fa, we realise, is barren but she has the overwhelming instinct to save "the new one" and mother it to maturity. Fa has the initiative to institute plans but they fail and she is lost in the waterfall. The new people fearing an onslaught of the devils flee in their dug-out canoes.

For the first time the angle of presentation changes and the final moments of Lok's life are described from the outside. He is like a specimen observed. He or it—as Lok is now referred to—returns to the scenes of the recent events and discovers what must be Liku's bones and the doll shaped like Oa. There is nothing left but to return to the shelter, lie down knees to chin with the little Oa figure before his face. It is then that the air is filled with the booming and crashing of the melting ice. In its fall it symbolises both the end of an ice-age and of the union with Oa.

The second change in the angle of presentation, which covers the whole final chapter, is reminiscent of the effect of the ending of *Lord of the Flies* in that we move from the ape-men to the new people and realise that our place is with them. The novel far from being a fantasy or merely a *tour de force* in imagining the workings of the pre-human mind is really directly about ourselves just as *Lord of the Flies* was as much about the adult world as it was about the boys. The passing of Lok and what he stands for emphasises the burden of human guilt and fear. This is the lesson that Tuami learns and he, if no others of his tribe, also begins to realise what his condition is. He becomes self-aware and able to see the possibilities of choice between good and evil.

The final tableau shows Tuami, the emerging leader

of the new people, with the survivors of the tribe making their way down to the sea away from the frightening dark forests full of "devils". One such "devil"—the baby ape-man—remains, suckled by Vivani. The memory of Liku and the guilt surrounding her survive as a nightmare in the brain of Tanakil.

Tuami is the representative new man in his violence and energy, in his skill as steersman, in his gifts of imagination which we see in the stag-dance, and in his drawings. He seeks too the imposition of his will, in particular in the coveting of Vivani who belongs to the old leader, Marlan. As he sits in the boat Tuami sharpens the blade of his ivory dagger and plans to usurp Marlan's position and murder him. He is also a philosopher and realises in a confused way that there is a shift in their experience; their escape is more than an escape. They have been thrust into a fearsome world:

> The world with the boat moving so slowly at the centre was dark amid the light, was untidy, hopeless, dirty. . . . They were as different from the group of bold hunters and magicians who had sailed up the river towards the fall as a soaked feather is from a dry one. Restlessly he turned the ivory in his hands. What was the use of sharpening it against a man? Who would sharpen a point against the darkness of the world?[8]

Violence seems to have yielded nothing except to confirm the darkness of the world. One can defeat men but not darkness. Tuami, the leader of the inheritors, is unsure of his heritage. For a moment confusion clears for Tuami and everything falls into place. In a moment of tension, frightened by the booming of the falling ice, the little ape-man appears with his rump in the air around Vivani's neck and everyone laughs, even the dourest of them. The token from the past and the latent love and acceptance the new people show as they play with the

[8] *Op. cit.*, pp. 225, 231.

little ape-man fuse in Tuami's mind and he realises the difference between good and evil:

> The sun shone on the head and the rump and quite suddenly everything was all right again and the sands had sunk back to the bottom of the pool. The rump and the head fitted each other and made a shape you could feel with your hands. They were waiting in the rough ivory of the knife-haft that was so much more important than the blade. They were an answer, the frightened, angry love of the woman and the ridiculous, intimidating rump that was wagging at her head, they were a password. His hands felt for the ivory in the bilges and he could feel in his fingers how Vivani and her devil fitted it.[9]

The book, however, does not end with such a positive and easy conclusion. The final picture is of a wandering group, facing a wide expanse of water, fleeing the darkness under the trees. There is nothing precise; in spite of his efforts Tuami "could not see if the line of darkness had an ending".

The point of the book lies in Tuami's self-knowledge which Golding throws into relief by showing how the security of Oa, too passive in its essence, must give way to a tormenting self-awareness, Tuami's and our own. This is the price that has to be paid for our humanity. The reader is put into the favoured position of knowing more of the dilemma than either Lok or Tuami could know and of seeing it in a more complex way. As Frank Kermode puts it: "Golding though he admits that we belong with the new man, supposes that we could not recapture that innocence, that natural veneration for Oa, the mother-goddess, had not something of it survived in us."[10] Golding is not saying either state is preferable or writing an elegy on the loss of Eden but using his characters to indicate two sides of our nature which con-

[9] *Op. cit.*, p. 233.

[10] F. Kermode, *op. cit.*, p. 14.

flict: a tolerant side which is passive, and an active side that cannot fail to hurt. His final position on the conflict of innocence and knowledge in *The Inheritors* is impartial. Two recent commentators on this novel see Tuami's lesson as the resolution of good and evil and interpret the end of the book as unequivocally a good beginning.[11] However, the tone of the final chapter suggests that though Tuami knows the difference between good and evil, though he knows that love is better than the point of a dagger, the future is undecided. The new beginning is perilous rather than good. If Tuami has the self-awareness to distinguish good and evil he has yet to practise it; his tolerance is only tentative. The evil he has become aware of arose, in fact, from the new men themselves and from nowhere else. "Evil enters the world through humanity and through no other creature" is Golding's own comment on this theme.[12]

Golding is careful even to the very last words to keep the reader's attention directed where he wants it. The novel is all the more forceful and moving because any thoughts of interpretation are created by the reactions it sets up in the reader. What one discovers is discovered obliquely. There is special aptness in the descriptions, nearly always successfully evoking the thinking patterns of the characters: ravens float in the air "like black scraps from a fire"; the unusual hair of the new men looks like "a rook's nest in a tall tree". There are many subtleties in the pattern of the book: the new men in their boat recall the dilemma of "the people" at the beginning of the novel; the ambivalence of Tuami's feelings in the boat is suggested by the contrast of the bright sunny morning and the darkness of the forests; we move with Lok from his playfulness to his touching, lonely, silent death and his silent tears for a state of being that

[11] M. Kinkead-Weekes and I. Gregor, *op. cit.*, p. 116.

[12] See O. Webster, "Living with Chaos", *Books and Art*, Mar. 1958, p. 15.

must inevitably pass away—we know what his tears mean as we know what Ralph's mean in *Lord of the Flies*. Golding is particularly successful in evoking a complex impression such as laughter in terms of primitive thinking by pictures or in providing parallels to describe exactly what the screaming of the captured Liku seemed like to Lok:

> The sounds made a picture in his head of interlacing shapes, thin, and complex, voluble and silly, not like the long curve of a hawk's cry, but tangled like line weed on the beach after a storm, muddled as water . . . Then among the laugh-sound on this side of the river Liku began to scream . . . The screaming tore him inside. It was not like the screaming of Fa when she was bearing the baby that died, or the mourning of Nil when Mal was buried; it was like the noise the horse makes when the cat sinks its curved teeth into the neck and hangs there, sucking blood.[13]

There are also numerous examples of carefully planned parallels that pay off richly and without strain: thus we see Lok and Fa, quite early on, innocently relishing the honey they find. Later they become intoxicated by it in the form of the fermented liquor that had been abandoned by the new people. In the grimly funny scene of Lok's drunkenness we begin to see the possibilities of evil invading the peaceful world of the ape-man. Lok imitates the behaviour of the new men and for the first time becomes violent with Fa.

Yet the objections to *The Inheritors* have been mainly stylistic and indeed there are places where the effort to maintain the angle of presentation causes some strain. At times the point of view shifts in too sophisticated a way for it to be acceptable as the thoughts of "the people":

[13] *T.I.*, pp. 104-5.

Fa and Lok considered the smoke without finding any picture they could share. There was smoke on the island, there was another man on the island. *There was nothing in life as a point of reference.*[14]

Or again:

The feeling inside him had sunk away and disappeared like the frost when the sun finds it on a flat rock. The people who were so miraculously endowed with possessions no longer seemed to him the immediate menace they had been earlier.[15]

The first sentence conveys exactly the way Lok understands but the second is too abstract in its language.

Sometimes too there are sentences that halt the reader:

The mud round Lok's ankles tightened so that he had to balance with his arms. *There was an astonishment in his head and beneath the astonishment a dull, heavy hunger that strangely included the heart.*[16]

More seriously, objections to the problem of finding a suitable language for "the people" and to the method of presentation whereby facts, such as the death of Liku, are withheld have led some critics to describe the book as a failure because of obscurity or because it bewilders the reader. Seen from this point of view Golding seems to receive more respect for his intention (generally highly praised) than his performance. This has led one critic to dismiss *The Inheritors* as "an over-simplifying fantasy"[17] and another to admire it a great deal "despite the mistaken literary strategy".[18]

Yet the strength of the novel *is* in its literary strategy.

[14] *Op. cit.*, p. 99.
[15] *Op. cit.*, p. 163.
[16] *Op. cit.*, p. 189.
[17] M. Walters: "Two fabulists: Golding and Camus", *Melbourne Critical Review*, No. 4, 1961, p. 24.
[18] John Wain, "Lord of the Agonies", *Aspect*, Apr. 1963, p. 59.

The convention of a language to convey "the people's" nonlinguistic experience, particularly the use of metaphor, can be and has been defended as not being an obstacle to the reader.[19] The originality is precisely in the imaginative projection of Lok's viewpoint through to Chapter 11 and the replacement of it in Chapter 12 by Tuami's, *i.e.* our own.

It is the concluding chapter and its implications that give the work its force. There is a logical and aesthetic progression towards it which fully justifies Golding's desire to make us see things his way first. Perhaps the subtlest balance in the book is the contrasting of emerging self-consciousness in Lok as much as in Tuami. The gap between the ape-men and the new people is not as clear-cut as it seems. Conflict, with the feeling of passivity in the veneration of Oa, begins to show in Fa and Ha, particularly in their curiosity and the attempt to apply their reason to specific situations and skills. It is a measure of Golding's success in character drawing that he brings off the feeling of touching ineffectualness in Lok's attempts to adapt himself to new situations. Lok becomes aware of an inside-Lok and an outside-Lok as a result of his observations of the new people and naïvely his attempt to understand them is to mime them. At its most grotesque this appears in his drunkenness where Fa is reduced to an object for beating. What Lok learns are all the negative things in the society of the new men; he can never hope to master their technological skills nor can he reach that clarity of understanding of his condition that Tuami achieves. In the end Lok must lose; he is so close still to Oa that he cannot survive in Tuami's world. In silent grief, dying in his foetal position, he underlines how much he is a child of earth. Yet Golding is not sentimentalising Lok and advocating a return to primeval innocence. He brings out the way in which the violent actions of the new men and the fate

[19] M. Kinkead-Weekes and I. Gregor, *op. cit.*, pp. 71-2.

of Lok's people are both inevitable. The reader is put clearly in the position of feeling both the need for self-assertion in the new men and the regret for that freedom from the burden of the self such as Lok and his kind know in relation to Oa.

CHAPTER IV

RECALCITRANCE: *PINCHER MARTIN*

The Inheritors, though it appears to be in form a "historical" novel, insulated from life as we know it, in fact expresses a general opinion on the human condition relevant to any period of human history. It is natural that after his evocation of the emergence of guilt in man Golding should feel drawn to considering particular instances in a modern social setting. This he has done both in *Pincher Martin* and *Free Fall*, but by contrasting procedures. With Pincher we are put in the position of considering his attitude to his death as illustated by his past behaviour. With Sammy, in *Free Fall*, we are presented not with a static character but with a developing one; we are led back into his past in an attempt to understand how he came to develop in the way he did and why he reacts as he does to the biggest crisis of his life.

The character of Pincher Martin, though perforce we learn of it in individual pieces, is cast in one block. The structure of the book, with its alternation between Pincher's "present" on the "rock" and the scenes from his past, might at first suggest a progression in understanding, a review of the past with an assessment of the lessons learned. In fact the past scenes, though culminating in a revelation, serve to underline the unwavering consistency of Pincher's behaviour and his attitude to himself and other people. The principal impression one receives of Pincher's character is his self-assertion whether in the tenacity of purpose behind his struggle for survival on the rock or in the imposition of his will on the people he knew and moved among in life. The book counterpoints the one kind of self-assertion against the other throughout until it comes to a startling and powerful resolution in the penultimate chapter. The contrast between Pincher in life and death shows him as petty, though grim, in the one and elevated to a lofty heroism in the other. The resolution will cut across both with its irony for any admiration we may have felt for his final raging against death is mistaken. Pincher is condemned for applying his energy to avoiding the admission of his essential nature, for not admitting to the evil in him, for not facing the darkness of his heart although he knows it exists. He comes to a point of self-awareness but will not capitulate.

The novel is narrated in an apparent "present" and concerns the struggle for survival of a drowning sailor in World War II, and his last days on a "rock" in the Atlantic. This immediacy is maintained through to the last chapter but one but in the final chapter the angle of presentation changes. In the present of actuality we find that Pincher Martin's putrefying body has been washed ashore and is being reclaimed by the Naval Authorities. The man who found the body worries whether Pincher suffered or not. The naval officer explains to him that this could hardly be so, since Pincher had not even had the time to kick off his sea-boots.

The effect of this trick ending is to make us realise either that Pincher was dead from almost the beginning of the novel or that the novel concerns his final moments of consciousness before death. In either case this ending must have a justification for its existence or else it would be pointless. It is a fact about the book that has caused argument ever since its appearance and some commentators have made very heavy weather of these sea-boots.[1] W. J. Harvey remarks: "Leaving aside the problem of evaluation, one finds a simple inability to under-

[1] See particularly W. Young, "Letter from London", *Kenyon Review*, Summer 1957.

stand."[2] Yet is there any real difficulty with the beginning of the book? Sufficient clues are given at the outset and others gradually assert themselves to prove to us, before Pincher himself will even admit it, that he is dead. The final words of the novel shock us out of the obsessive but non-existent physical world Pincher creates for himself and stress the fact that the real concern of the book has been with spiritual torment.

The reader is obliged, as he approaches the opening for the first time, to interpret it as Pincher's final conscious thoughts. There are two points that establish themselves. He first utters "Moth-" which is traditionally accepted as the last thought of a drowning man and then envisages in his mind the picture of a little glass figure in a jam jar whose movements can be controlled by pressure on a rubber membrane cover. It is characteristic of Pincher to cancel the self-less cry of "Mother" and replace it with an image that illustrates the controlling and directing of the self:

> Could he have controlled the nerves of his face, or could a face have been fashioned to fit the attitude of his consciousness where it lay suspended between life and death that face would have worn a snarl . . . . The hard lumps of water no longer hurt. There was a kind of truce, observation of the body. There was no face but there was a snarl.
>
> A picture steadied and the man regarded it . . .
>
> The jam jar was standing on a table, brightly lit from O.P. It might have been a huge jar in the centre of a stage or a small one almost touching the face, but it was interesting because one could see into a little world there which was quite separate but which one could control. The jar was nearly full of clear water and a tiny glass figure floated upright in it. The top of

[2] W. J. Harvey, "The Reviewing of Contemporary Fiction", *Essays in Criticism*, Apr. 1958, p. 184.

the jar was covered with a thin membrane—white rubber. He watched the jar without moving or thinking while his distant body stilled itself and relaxed . . . By varying the pressure on the membrane you could do anything you liked with the glass figure which was wholly in your power.[3]

By this time Pincher is already dead and the reader is obliged to accept that fact and assume Pincher is in some kind of after-life. The difficulty lies in the way the text moves from establishing Pincher's last living thoughts in the present to extending them into the "suspended present" of the remainder of the novel, where we are in fact concerned with Pincher's future in hell.

"The delicate balance of the glass figure related itself to his body. In a moment of wordless realisation he saw himself touching the surface of the sea with just such a dangerous stability, poised between floating and going down. The snarl thought words to itself . . .

Of course, My lifebelt.

It was bound by tapes under that arm and that, etc.[4]

To ask that Golding should have said quite baldly at the beginning: here is a drowned sailor and this is what his hell is like, would be to miss the particular value the experience of reading the book provides. It is not as simple as saying that from the moment of extinction we pass over into a purgatory ready for heaven or hell. The hell or heaven provided is of our own making and gradually we learn that Pincher Martin represents the power of the self established to such an extreme that it will not concede the passing over to a state it cannot control. We move after the drowning into Pincher's death-state which the author has legitimately contrived to present as an alleged consciousness for the purpose of allowing us to discover how Pincher fashions his own hell on the

[3] *P.M.*, pp. 8-9. [4] *Op. cit.*, p. 9.

model of his past life. Upon reflexion we see that Pincher's last thought of the figure in the jar is his instinctive and typical reaction towards looking after number one: an invention of his imagination to protect himself even in death, an attempt to escape death by imitating the "dangerous stability" of the bobbing figure. It is obviously of more value for Golding to establish this important feature of Pincher's character than just to say flatly that he is dead. The idea of an undeviating will must arise organically from the narration and with it comes the advantage of a dramatic irony in that the reader is placed in the superior position of knowing that Pincher's will cannot succeed this time. Pincher does eventually realise that his clever inventions are illusory and that he can no longer avoid facing the truth that living for the self has led to the evil of using other people as things. Yet he refuses to admit it and the force of this refusal comes across only through the illusion of Pincher carrying over the self-will of life into death. This is the justification for the opening of the book, and for the final chapter too. We are made to realise that Pincher did not suffer in body, even though his corpse is a repulsive mess, since he did not even have the time to kick off his sea-boots. The book has dealt with his suffering in spirit.

The climax of his suffering is his confrontation with God who appears to him as a face, the nearest possible emblem to a humanity that Pincher has constantly denied. The preparation for this is both skillful and compelling. Numerous counter rhythms are set up in the reader. At times he is drawn into and completely absorbed by Pincher's meticulous efforts to save his skin and establish himself on the rock in order to wait for rescue. This is the result of a very cunningly used naturalistic style that convinces the reader of the very feel of water and rock and the acuteness of Pincher's pain. One remembers barnacles oozing uretic water, anemones out of the tide described as slumped breasts with the milk drawn from them, the piercing sweetness of a single grain of chocolate, or the "faint scratching sound of oilskin as the body shivered". At other times the reader is not observing Pincher from outside but impressionistically experiencing what it is like inside Pincher's skull looking out from under the arches of his brow. The feeling of actuality on the rock contrasts with the flashbacks to real life in which Pincher appears in all his pettiness, nastiness, selfishness, murderousness. On the rock, however, he reveals his amazing ingenuity in adjusting himself to his surroundings, devising incredible solutions for enormous problems so that he takes on the heroic stature of Atlas, Ajax, Prometheus, Lear. The projection of Pincher onto a cosmic scale is suggested quite early on. He thinks of himself as inhabiting a crevice (his body) like the outer crevice of the rock:

> He himself was at the far end of this inner crevice of flesh. At this far end, away from the fires, there was a mass of him lying on a lifebelt that rolled backwards and forwards at every breath. Beyond the mass was the round, bone globe of the world and himself hanging inside.[5]

As Pincher progresses in mastery of the rock we realise before he does, from various clues, that he is bound for a terrible disappointment. His imagination has been too clever so that his invention of incredible evasion begins to crack. He sees a red lobster in the sea and does not realise at first what his mistake is; he remembers that guano is insoluble so the pain in his eye that he had thought of as caused by the slimy water in his trench cannot come from an outside agency; the familiarity of his rock, and its resemblance to a tooth, is finally explained by the admission that everything he has invented has centred on the memory of an aching tooth in his

[5] *Op. cit.*, pp. 48-9.

own jaw.[6] Pincher is at last turned in upon his own mind and begins the final part of his ordeal. He cannot escape outwards to a rock or rescue because neither is there. He is left facing his own essential self.

The final part of Pincher's torment is conveyed in a powerful converging of the metaphors used throughout the novel. Pincher's actions are explained through the overlapping metaphors of drowning, eating, and acting and his dilemma in the death-state by the images of a "centre" and the "darkness".

To begin with, what could be a more illuminating image of self for self than the struggling of a drowning man? Struggle he must and preserve himself somehow he must, but these automatic reflexes also tally with Pincher's character and coincide with the best moment in his career to illustrate the kind of life he has led. He has always thought of himself as special, precious. He is a man who can say "I'm going to have a damned long life and get what I'm after" and mean it. His appetite must always be satisfied. Part of his torment on the rock is hunger and making do with the thought of eating which he is at last able to place in a wider context:

> And of course eating with the mouth was only the gross expression of what was a universal process. You could eat with your cock or with your fists, or with your voice.[7]

The flashbacks show us Pincher's unpleasant determination never to miss an opportunity, never to be the loser in the game. The game for him is consume or be consumed. In civilian life Pincher had been an actor and on one occasion he had been called upon to double the parts of a shepherd and one of the seven deadly sins. His reputation in the company earns him the mask of Greed

[6] The clues for this piece of conclusive evidence can be traced as follows: pp. 24, 30, 77, 78, 91, 125, 129, 174.

[7] *P.M.*, p. 88.

which fits him perfectly. One of the actors jokingly introduces Greed to Pincher and Pincher to Greed:

> He takes the best part, the best seat, the most money, the best notice, the best woman. He was born with his mouth and his flies open and both hands out to grab. He's a cosmic case of the bugger who gets his penny and someone else's bun.[8]

Christopher Martin, like Dusty Miller or Nobby Clark, acquires his lower-deck nickname—Pincher—automatically and aptly. Pincher knows you can grab and consume in more ways than one. And he has done it. He cuckolds a colleague and makes sure he witnesses it; he uses a young boy in a passionless homosexual affair; he courts the producer's wife so as to get the best parts in the company; he is not above maiming a friend who is speeding past him on his motorbike; he attempts to seduce Mary, later to be his best friend's fiancée, and because of her refusal to crash the car they are travelling in; above all, he tries to murder his best friend, Nat, by giving a helm-order that will swerve the boat and throw him overboard.

In his world of consume or be consumed action and assertiveness are the greatest advantages. If there is any obstacle Pincher is in no doubt what to do—eat your opponent. His attitude is illustrated by the story of the Chinese custom of burying a fish in a tin box and letting it be consumed by maggots until at first there are are only two fat maggots left and then only one, even fatter. In the final event of Pincher's life Pincher has cast himself in the role of one of the maggots and his friend Nat in the other. Nat is a saint-like person who hides away aft, from the crew, in order to pray. Pincher has known him as a student and is familiar with his definition of heaven:

[8] *Op. cit.*, p. 120.

> Take us as we are now and heaven would be sheer negation. Without form and void. You see? A sort of black lightning destroying everything that we call life.[9]

Nat admires Pincher's tenacity, the quality needed in Nat's opinion to achieve the technique of what he calls "dying into heaven". The dilemma for Pincher is that he both loves Nat and hates him. He hates him in the first instance from jealousy because of Mary, the girl who had refused his advances; more deeply her impregnability and attachment to Nat are a challenge to his pride, his precious self. Ironically, as Nat suggests, people are blended together more than they think. It is Pincher who introduces Mary to Nat and who is to be best man. Pincher's self-centred nature and Nat's natural goodness are complementary. Pincher's tenacity and drive, combined with Nat's goodness, would best achieve the technique of "dying into heaven".

As things are Pincher sees his opportunity to get rid of Nat. On the bridge of the destroyer he takes the initiative and gives a helm-order, as if to avoid a bit of wreckage. This throws Nat who is "at his aeons", praying aft in a dangerous position, overboard. "Goodbye, Nat, I loved you and it is not in my nature to love much. But what can the last maggot but one do? Lose his identity?" The imposition of the will is always effective but not always just. The last bitter laugh is on Pincher since the order, given seconds earlier, would have been the right initiative to take to avoid the torpedo that sinks the ship. The self has missed its chance of heroic glory, though if it had succeeded Nat would have been its victim. This order, both willed and necessary as Frank Kermode has described it,[10] separates Nat and Pincher for ever and in doing that destroys any possible balance between natural goodness and undeviating selfishness.

[9] *Op. cit.*, p. 70.

[10] *Cf.* Frank Kermode: "The Novels of William Golding", *International Literary Annual*, vol. iii, 1961, p. 24.

The spring for the finale is the surrender of reason. Pincher has used reason as a means of asserting himself, of trying to prove to himself that all is under control, that he is winning. He works out a plan of survival, deciding what limited practical things can be done—get food, avoid illness, keep a grip on actuality. To this end he has found some meagre food and, to help his rescue, erected a small stone figure and spread out sea-weed as signals to a passing ship or plane. He names his territory: the place where he eats is The Red Lion, three rocky projections are Oxford Circus, Piccadilly, and Leicester Square. He thinks mind is master of all, a tool to be used in imposing his will. The rock is something to be tamed, to be adapted to his own ways:

> I will impose my routine on it, my geography. I will tie it down with names . . . I will use my brain as a delicate machine-tool to produce the results I want.[11]

He uses reason as the mainstay in evading having to face his essential self. Even sleep, he thinks, can be controlled by it, yet he cannot sleep to order. He is afraid to; it is an area best left untouched:

> There the carefully hoarded and enjoyed personality, our only treasure and at the same time our only defence must die into the ultimate truth of things[12] . . .

What Pincher is afraid of being reduced to is the "centre", the image used to describe the irreducible in him, the essential self that knows all about external actions and desires. It is an element so essentially at the centre of things that it cannot even examine itself: "in the darkness of the skull, it existed, a darker dark, self-existent and indestructible."[13] The centre is tireless in the assertion of its presence; it is the thing Pincher's will refuses to acknowledge. But cracks begin to form in the

[11] *P.M.*, pp. 86-7. [12] *Op. cit.*, p. 91.
[13] *Op. cit.*, p. 45.

defences of reason. He remembers childhood nightmares of the inescapable darkness of the cellars. His attempt to avoid going back to this runs parallel to avoiding the centre. Darkness and centre coincide and a pattern emerges that Pincher is not sure of but whose effect is to make reason falter. He makes one last attempt to assert control; if he is ill he must be constipated and reason can solve that by applying an enema by means of the inner tube of his lifebelt:

> All the terrors of hell can come down to nothing more than a stoppage. Why drag in good and evil when the serpent lies coiled in my own body?[14]

He imagines he is victor by expelling the poison in him. The description of the enema to an orchestral accompaniment, culminating in the intricate glory of a cadenza, is grimly funny. The exaggeration proves a point against Pincher. This purging of evil is still not the acknowledgment of it; it is another evasion. Hallucinations begin: the rock moves, a red lobster swims in the sea. He has a blackout, a crisis that marks a difference between previous experience and a new experience. Up to this point the novel has fluctuated between phases of a morning and an evening right up to the fifth day. There is no sixth. Pincher has emerged from the chaos of water, made his earth of a rock, mastered it, named it, and filled it but there the power of his will ends. The final effort, which is to create himself, fails. The first five days are not preliminaries to the creation of man but Pincher's method of evading the essential ingredient of man: the fact that he must at one point at least face the centre, the truth about himself. Pincher is brought unequivocally to admit what is happening: the dark represents the truth about him that he has tried to avoid but also a power beyond him that he cannot control, an existence greater than self that he will not acknowledge.

[14] *Op. cit.*, p. 163.

Pincher still does anything rather than concede even if all he can hang on to is mechanical reflexes. He talks, eats, contemplates the waves. He keeps his body and his senses occupied in the hope of avoiding facing what the centre wants him to admit. He conveniently splits himself into body and mind as a means of self-protection: "I was always two things, mind and body. Nothing has altered." He oscillates between mouth and centre, between talk as a subterfuge and the obligation to face the truth, the darkness in the cellar:

> Out of bed on the carpet with no shoes . . . forced to go down to meet the thing I turned my back on . . . Coffin ends crushed in the wall. Under the churchyard back through the death door to meet the master . . . Pattern repeated from the beginning of time . . . The cellar door swinging to behind a small child who must go down in his sleep to meet the thing he turned from when he was created.[15]

The quacking mouth cannot fool the centre. In the final hallucination, where God appears as a face, Pincher's mouth continues to assert its defiance. On Pincher's terms man created God on the sixth day and can go on to create his own heaven. To which the answer of the face is that Pincher has created it. Pincher justifies his living for self and prefers it to God's mercy. As he sees it he would, whatever the circumstances of his life, have found himself on that same bridge, giving the same helm-order—at once right and wrong.

Yet, suppose I climbed away from the cellar over the

[15] *Op. cit.*, pp. 178, 179, 189. *Cf.* "The Ladder and the Tree" in *H.G.* and Golding's explanation that the cellar image "represents more than childhood terrors; a whole philosophy in fact—suggesting that God is the thing we turn away from into life, and therefore we hate and fear him and make a darkness there," quoted by J. Peter in *William Golding's L.F. A Source book*, ed. William Nelson, New York 1963, p. 34.

> bodies of used and defeated people, broke them to make steps on the road away from you, why should you torture me? If I ate them, who gave me a mouth?[16]

The mouth rejects God: "I spit on your compassion." When there is no more mouth the centre itself resists: "I shit on your heaven." It rejects the challenge of facing the darkness, of admitting man can beome self-aware and know the source of evil in himself which is a necessary part of his creation. To admit the evil in human nature would be the surest destruction of Pincher's world and this he will not allow. All that is left of Pincher is his hands like lobster claws and the centre, a recalcitrant centre—two forms of defence.

Pincher knows he should admit the knowledge of his evil, his darkness, but he will not. Man is on the run from a primeval dark thing. He cannot help his selfishness and his appetites. They are his driving force in life; they affirm his existence and also confirm him in the task of avoiding having to return to the dark place in the cellar. Like the new men in *The Inheritors* Pincher shows how the affirmation of the self is equated with the perilous process of living; like Tuami he knows the difference between good and evil. The flashbacks to his life illustrate the dilemma of a modern Tuami who knows he must go forward and turn his back on the dark forests.

The rejection of the darkness can only be postponed; there comes a time when the resolution of the evil in our nature has to be accepted and the self become self-less. Loss of self—a return to the dark place in the cellar—is what Pincher will not accept. What is tragic is that even if he does not return he must know that he is forever denying part of the truth and he is incomplete. He must either confront the frightening dark or else torture himself endlessly in a heaven (or hell) of his own making. True to character Pincher remains stubborn. Stubborn

[16] *P.M.*, p. 197.

but wrong. The lightning, the force of God, does not give up. It worries at the dead man's hands, now become claws, in order to find a crack in the defences; it bides its time for access to the centre:

> The lightning came forward. Some of the lines pointed to the centre, waiting for the moment when they could pierce it. Others lay against the claws, playing over them, prying for a weakness, wearing them away in a compassion that was timeless and without mercy.[17]

Pincher Martin is certainly a difficult book to understand but its difficulties are necessary to its structure, and to the kind of experience Golding is trying to communicate. He has in fact accepted that it is a difficult book and has provided a plain statement on the self-centred character of Pincher.[18] On the question of Pincher's freedom of choice, to centre the world on himself, he has also explained how Pincher inevitably creates not only his own world but his own hell:

> . . . you meet a Christian—he thinks that when he dies he will either have devils with three-pronged forks and forked tails or angels with wings and palms. If you're not a Christian and die, then if the universe is as the Christian sees it, you will still go either to heaven or hell or purgatory. But your purgatory or your heaven or your hell won't have the Christian attributes . . . They'll be things that you make yourself, that's all there is to it. And that Pincher was a pincher. He'd spent the whole of his life acquiring things that really belonged to other people, and bit by bit they were taken away from him in purgatory, till he ended as what he was.[19]

[17] *Op. cit.*, p. 201.
[18] Quoted by Frank Kermode *op. cit.*
[19] See Frank Kermode, Interview with Golding for BBC, 28 Aug. 1959.

Part of the achievement of the novel is the way we are completely engaged not only by the power of Pincher to mould his world but also by the energy that is carried over into his death-state. Golding's novel can in this respect be compared with Ambrose Bierce's short-story, "An Occurrence at Owl Creek Bridge" which may have suggested the device of a hero, apparently alive, who communicates to us the hyper-intensity of his experience. Peyton Farquhar—the scene is set during the American Civil War—is to be hanged from the bridge: but we learn that like Pincher he was dead from the beginning of the story. The snapping rope, the illusion of escape, and the return home are therefore a poignant evocation of his very last seconds of life. Bierce aims, by his trick ending, to heighten this poignancy, Golding to put Pincher's character in perspective. Bierce gains our sympathy for Peyton Farquhar but does not use his last moments to judge him or get us to judge him. The trick ending in neither case is unacceptable. Both use it legitimately: to convey the pointlessness of the execution in Bierce's case and more profoundly in Golding's to judge and condemn Pincher's self-centredness.

If Bierce's story was at the back of his mind and suggested a structural device to him[20] Golding has certainly carried it much further both with the intention of making *Pincher Martin* deliberately explicit and at the same time of heightening the mythical stature of Pincher as representative of fallen man:

> I said to myself: "Now here is going to be a novel, it's going to be a blow on behalf of the ordinary universe,

[20] *Cf.* B. S. Oldsey and S. Weintraub, *The Art of William Golding*, New York 1965, p. 77. *Cf.* also I. Blake, "*P.M.*—William Golding and Taffrail", *Notes & Queries*, August 1962,who suggests that Golding may have got more than the name from Taffrail's *Pincher Martin O.D.* By a process of reaction, as in the case of *L.F.*, Golding rejects the bland assurance of Taffrail that his Pincher simply commended his soul to his maker.

> which I think on the whole likely to be the right one, and I'm going to write it so vividly and accurately and with such an exact programme that nobody can possibly mistake exactly what I mean . . . (Pincher is) very much fallen—he's fallen more than most. In fact, I went out of my way to damn Pincher as much as I could by making him the most unpleasant, the nastiest type I could think of, and I was very interested to see how critics all over the place said, "Well yes, we are like that."[21]

Golding's intention is clear enough: to invent a character who is both grandiose and mean, ordinary yet possessing the stature of myth. Opinion seems to have been evenly divided both on the execution and on the question: is Pincher hero or villain? On the one hand *Pincher Martin* has received the highest praise for its "total technical control" where there is no distinguishing "between a compassion that might be called religious and the skill of an artist; they are the same thing".[22] On the other there are frequent reservations about the overexplicitness of the "story's doctrinal arc"[23] or the virtuosity working in a void,[24] the result being to cancel the effectiveness of Pincher as a character who is considered to be either not novelistically treated or simply uninteresting. Both views are hard to accept when one remembers that the novel, though on one level concerned with spiritual torment in a hypothetical after-life, has as its terms of reference ordinary living. Pincher's life may be sketchy, perhaps unsubtle, but it is plausible and acceptable as representing a certain type of experience. Why should Pincher be considered uninteresting? He is petty certainly but the universality of his behaviour is made more acceptable in its banality than it would be if it were extravagantly

[21] BBC Interview. [22] Frank Kermode, *op. cit.*, p. 25.
[23] John Wain, "Lord of the Agonies", *Aspect*, Apr. 1963, p. 62.
[24] W. J. Harvey, *op. cit.*, p. 185.

beyond normal possibilities. What Pincher does is undesirable but not so exceptional. The objection that "a ship-wrecked sailor is interesting only if *he* is interesting"[25] simply begs the question. Indeed the general claim has been that in spite of the author Pincher takes on our unwilling sympathy like Milton's Satan and is too heroic to be crushed. Golding, it is clear, has the opposite intention; Pincher is in his view undeniably wrong. It is not Milton's Satan he should be compared to but rather Wagner's Alberich in *The Ring*. Like him Pincher is consistently evil. What then makes the book—as no one has denied—compelling reading if the author's point is so explicit? It is surely that Golding hits on the tragic in Pincher and the ordinariness of his tragedy—Pincher is quite unable to repent, he simply cannot help resisting. His doubtful virtue is recalcitrance. His grandeur is very tawdry; irony takes care of that.

[25] F. Karl, *A Reader's Guide to the Contemporary English Novel*, London 1962, p. 259.

CHAPTER V

BODY AND SOUL: *FREE FALL*

Both Pincher Martin and Sammy Mountjoy are held in the tormenting vice of the self, and their further torment is to come to know this. For Pincher the experience operates in very special conditions; his defiant self can do no more than hold out in a rearguard action. His self-knowledge is certainly too late. For Sammy in *Free Fall* it may also be too late but he has survived his ordeal and can speak of it. He can also claim to have been transfigured by it and this is the Sammy who tells us in his own words how his understanding of the world and of his own life has been altered. It is this new Sammy who opens his confession-cum-apologia with ecstatic prose which conveys both his exultation and his determination to examine himself:

> I have walked by stalls in the market-place where books, dog-eared and faded from their purple, have burst with a white hosanna . . . I have felt the flake of fire fall, miraculous and pentecostal. My yesterdays walk with me. They keep step, they are grey faces that peer over my shoulder.[1]

The search Sammy embarks upon is a personal one and, by the nature of things, a not very coherent one. Golding justifies the particular order of events, deliberately dislocated from a strict time sequence, by his desire to show "the patternlessness of life before we impose our patterns on it".[2] Sammy is searching for the precise moment

[1] *F.F.*, p. 5.

[2] See O. Webster, "Living with Chaos", *Books and Art*, Mar. 1958, p. 15.

when innocence was lost, when choosing became no longer free but limited by circumstances which in turn further limited future choices. He has known the freedom of choice and realises it cannot be explained; it has to be experienced, as he says, like a colour or the taste of potatoes. He is seeking a pattern that explains his experience as it presents itself to him rather than as something that can be neatly fitted into an existing system. Finding an all-inclusive explanation for "the decision made freely that cost me my freedom" is what Sammy really hankers after, self-understanding even more than his art. He is a successful painter with work in the Tate but his art is not enough. This is why he claims he would sooner be good than clever. He demands the privilege of presenting things in his order without regard for chronological sequence. Sammy wants a full confession, not an aesthetic arrangement. Deeper still he seeks to understand the innermost core of his motives, the innermost knowledge, his innermost darkness:

> It is the unnameable, unfathomable and invisible darkness that sits at the centre of him, always awake . . . that hopes hopelessly to understand and be understood. Our loneliness is the loneliness not of the cell or the castaway; it is the loneliness of that dark thing that sees as at the atom furnace by reflection . . .[3]

Where to begin? Ecstasy leads to enquiry and enquiry begins with childhood. He knows childhood has an innocence, a freedom from responsibility, all its own. If he had committed murder then it would have been of no consequence: but he begins there, nevertheless, for the help the contrast will yield between "the little boy, clear as spring water, and the man like a stagnant pool".

His infancy in the twenties in Rotten Row, a rural slum south of London, is marked by squalor and dirt both in the physical conditions of life and in morals.

[3] *F.F.*, p. 8.

Sammy is illegitimate and his Ma, for all her boozy warmth and naturalness, a whore. The emphasis on crude physicality, particularly of Ma and the girl Evie who first takes Sammy to school, serves to contrast with his awareness of the bliss of this life. There is no evil in Ma and Evie for all the dirt.

He has two friends while in the elementary school: Johnny and Philip. Johnny is clever at mechanical things and knows all about planes. He will embrace the physical side of life without complications. Sammy has a memory of him later in the novel whizzing by on his motor-bike and kissing the girl behind him in carefree joy. Philip is more complex; his need to protect himself against the toughs has made him Machiavellian. There is the element of the exploiter in him; he knows about people and can use them. He is "clever, complex, never a child".

The memories of games with Johnny release certain qualities of Sammy's mind. The memories are less important than the way they prompt his awareness of a search for self-knowledge: "the beginning of responsibility, the beginning of darkness, the point where I began." With Philip he has a foretaste of what it is like to be exploited. Sammy's infatuation for collecting fag-cards of the Kings of Egypt leads to Philip's suggestion that Sammy should waylay boys in the lavatory and fight them for their cards, Sammy taking the Kings and giving the others to him. The scheme results in one card for Sammy and twenty for Philip. The second prank is a bigger temptation. Philip dares Sammy to urinate on the church altar. In the event he can only spit dryly, is caught in the act, and receives a clout on the ear. The immediate result is the breaking of his mastoid and his stay in hospital. At the death of Ma he is adopted by the withdrawn and slightly mad Rector of the church.

This is the end of an era, the end of "the infant Samuel". The operation for the mastoid leaves a scar but the scar makes new flesh. There is no guilt there, the boy is absolved. It was a time of happiness because of being unconscious of happiness. The moment of self-awareness—yet to be fixed—will be the moment of the end of innocence and the origin of all subsequent acts and attitudes. The process of living brings Sammy inevitably nearer to this moment of responsibility. The test of his character will be the way he negotiates this critical point and the kind of choice he makes. Two choices will be open to him—a fuller one which involves the subjection of part of himself and a narrower one that allows his self-will full rein but with diminishing returns.

In the second phase of the story that Sammy presents to us he is in pursuit of Beatrice Ifor. It is during the years just before World War II and they are both nineteen. Sammy is at an art school and Beatrice at a training college. He is aware that by this time of his life the moment of responsibility he is looking for has passed. His freedom has almost entirely gone and he is committed to a certain sequence of choices stemming from that moment. These choices culminate in, at first, the chaste wooing of Beatrice, then in a sort of engagement, and finally in Beatrice's complete subjection to him.

Beatrice is a symbol of the unknown and Sammy's love for her is really a form of jealousy, a need to bring into his own orbit something that challenges him from outside. His feelings are mixed; at first he wants to protect, not exploit. In intention he would like to be unselfish and honourable but he falls victim to selfishness. This fall is a choice consequent on an earlier one, that very choice which is the origin of all his choices and that he has not yet isolated. His generous thoughts belong to the period when Beatrice is carnally removed from him. Will he be as unselfish before the flesh? In his urge to express his love for her he wants to know what it is like to be Beatrice. His confession of love is "I want to be you" which betrays a determination to possess rather than a desire to call out a reciprocal feeling. He makes progress with Beatrice but strictly chastely. After four years she succumbs but there is no great delight in it. The first occasion is a failure for Sammy—though he has had an affair—and the subsequent ones unrewarding. Sammy before the flesh loses his good intentions because of Beatrice's lack of response, because she settles for less and is satisfied to have Sammy as her tower and let herself be the ivy clinging to it. There is a contrast between the ideal in Sammy's mind and the reality that suggests a realistic view of the Dante-Beatrice situation. Love is not shared but made into an exploitation, an infliction. Bored with Beatrice he abandons her for a girl called Taffy who has as natural an appetite for love and sex as Beatrice's was grudging. He marries Taffy and there is a child. He justifies his rejection of Beatrice as the inexorable workings of a machine. He describes the reaction of his nature as mechanical and helpless. These are the consequences of a decision. He has still to locate the moment of that decision.

The third phase of the story takes place during the war. Sammy, well able to look after number one, has avoided the fighting and become a war-artist. He is a p.o.w. and is being interrogated about the escape of two fellow-officers from the camp. Sammy, though still not clear of the moment of decision he is searching for, is aware at least of how he acquired the capacity to understand. It was through Dr Halde, his interrogator, who as part of the process of breaking down his victim perceptively begins to reveal Sammy to himself. He reveals to him first his mediocrity:

> You do not believe in anything enough to suffer for it or be glad . . . You wait in a dusty waiting-room on no particular line for no particular train. And between the poles of belief, I mean the belief in material things and the belief in a world made and supported by a

> supreme being, you oscillate jerkily from day to day. from hour to hour.[4]

This part of Halde's softening up process ends with his tempting Sammy with a promise of freedom; like Satan he has taken him to a pinnacle of the temple and offered him all he could want. Halde is only using the reference figuratively: but to continue the figure Sammy should answer categorically in the negative. Sammy cannot give an absolute answer either way. At this point in his story Sammy is still very ordinary and reacts by dithering over the possible arguments on either side. This is not the transformed Sammy we have already met with his apocalyptic unrelenting language. That change is yet to come. At the moment Sammy cannot answer because he is genuinely confused about the whole issue of interrogation. Sammy knows nothing because he was never trusted with anything by his comrades: but, relatively speaking, he does know something by surmise and could name twenty-odd men involved in the escape-plot. Since he has no experience of an absolute he begins to justify himself by reference to the wide relative spectrum of events. This is Halde's second revelation—Sammy's confusion amid relative values:

> I could see this war as the ghastly and ferocious play of children who having made a wrong choice or a whole series of them were now hopelessly tormenting each other because a wrong use of freedom had lost them their freedom. Everything was relative, nothing absolute.[5]

Sammy has lived in the drabness of mediocrity and deceived himself by the convenience of relative arguments. Logically, in the circumstances he is now in, he must capitulate to Halde and equally logically speak his relative truth: he cannot be certain of an absolute. He is

[4] *Op. cit.*, p. 144. [5] *Op. cit.*, p. 150.

forced to admit that he is not sure whether he knows anything or not. Halde is not satisfied and Sammy is put blindfolded in solitary confinement.

Sammy's first problem is to get used to the blindfold because of his fear of the dark. With the removal of the blindfold his problem is intensified and enlarged. He finds he is in a blacked out cell and instead of being handed over to his torturers, as he thought, he is alone, ready to torture himself. His fear has already begun. With no belt for his trousers he has to hold them up, not for decency but protection. The essential thing for Sammy seems to be his sex.

Sammy is in a state of doubt, pared down ready for an illumination. Halde is unaware of the service he is doing Sammy. He has brought him to a state of doubt which will be the springboard to a state of absolute self-knowledge. Using his sense impressions—his only tools, and limited at that—Sammy discovers his black world. By getting his back into the corners he establishes the shape of his darkness. But the walls of his cell are relatively stable elements in his system of knowledge. The unknown that remains forever impenetrable is somewhere in the centre of the cell. There is something there which causes the greatest fear, some wet, slimy object that Sammy persuades himself must be part, perhaps the most essential physical part, of a man. He is powerless to escape his torment. He knows where the door is—a wooden one—yet he refuses to tackle it. To step out would only be to return to Halde and the camp, another prison. He is made aware of the impotence of his will. Sammy's torment builds up to unbearability because of the centre of the cell, the centre of the darkness. He creates by sense perceptions the image of some sexual object which is equated in turn with that irreducible element in the darkness which is the essential self. In terror Sammy cries out for help though resigned to despair and experiences gratuitously a spiritual rebirth at the very moment his physical energy hurls itself on the door and breaks through.

The result of Sammy's self-knowledge is to see things not as relative but as unique yet integrated. Ironically the method that helped him towards his absolute ecstatic vision was, while in the dark cell, the logical sequence of sense information provided by touch. All that had existed for Sammy was physical, now all is transfigured and exists on a spiritual level:

> Huge tears were dropping from my face into dust; and this dust was a universe of brilliant and fantastic crystals, that miracles instantly supported in their being . . . Those crowded shapes extending up into the air and down into the rich earth, those deeds of far space and deep earth were aflame at the surface and daunting by right of their own natures though a day before I should have disguised them as trees. Beyond them the mountains were not only clear all through like purple glass, but living. They sang and were conjubilant. They were not all that sang. Everything is related to everything else and all relationship is either discord or harmony. The power of gravity, dimension and space, the movement of the earth and sun and unseen stars, these made what might be called music and I heard it.[6]

In this moving climactic piece of Traherne-like prose Golding prepares the way for the conclusions Sammy is to draw from his experience. Sammy and Pincher here show their similarity and divergence. Both have led banal lives yet both have extraordinary spiritual experiences. The interesting thing in Sammy's case will be to see how he can act on his experience. *Pincher Martin* is concerned with eschatology; Sammy's case is more specific and testable.

What meaning can ecstatic illumination have in real life? To his fellow-officers Sammy's ecstasy may be an

[6] *Op. cit.*, pp. 186-7.

embarrassment but he himself is aware of his "complete and luminous sanity". He discovers in himself a "vital morality" that understands people as people. It is the beginning of the collapse of Sammy's self-deception. His vision has made life more worthwhile yet more difficult for him, almost unendurable. He cannot accept his revelation complacently. It forces him to appreciate the "natural generosity" of Johnny and regret the absence of it in himself. He is aware at least of the fullness of Beatrice as a human being as opposed to the beautiful and unresponsive object he had imagined—or created her—as. Yet once involved with her he could not have prevented the course of events. However, there was also a time of freedom when he was not a victim of contingent circumstances. It was like the taste of potatoes, not an abstraction but tasted, known. He has proved to himself that the moment of choice was not in childhood nor in manhood. Then it must have been during late adolescence.

In the fourth phase of the novel we return to Sammy's schooldays and discover the origins of his outlook on life. The ideas "the earnest metaphysical boy" imbibes present him with a difficult twofold problem. The lessons he most favours and with which he has the most affinities are imparted by the cruelly sarcastic Miss Rowena Pringle, an excessively fastidious and crabbed spinster, who teaches Scripture. The science lessons, on the other hand, and their rationalist basis, Sammy appreciates but realises are limited. These are taught by Nick Shales, clever, tolerant, and likeable. The children go from Miss Pringle's vivid Bible stories, including the one about Moses and the burning bush, straight to Nick's classes on the conservation of energy, and accept them both. The contradiction in Nick's nature is that he is quite selfless yet preaches the gospel of a dreary mechanistic universe. As for Miss Pringle, the nasty streak in her turns Sammy from her teaching though it is the world of miracles she describes that he would naturally prefer. He chooses to accept Nick's exact universe where "you can't have your penny and your bun", where the law of conservation of energy holds good on a mental as well as a physical level. He makes his choice on the personalities of his teachers, a choice between the physical and the spiritual, between body and soul. He describes his choice as a door slamming shut on Moses and Jehovah, not to be opened again until his experience in the Nazi prison camp.

Yet this is not the moment of choice that occasions all others. But at last Sammy comes near it as he approaches the sexuality of late adolescence. Beatrice is a girl in the drawing class and she happens to be posing as a portrait model. Sammy is not particularly interested and does a quick but, so it turns out, excellent sketch for his friend Philip just to help him since Philip has no talent at all. Philip signs it and everyone thinks it is his, including Beatrice who is flattered. The sketch reveals to Sammy how much more involved he is than he thought and it is ironical that in his selfless expression in the drawing he has been exploited by the wily Philip. Further attempts to capture Beatrice, in drawing, fail and she takes on the suggestion of a challenge, a challenge to Sammy's existence. It is more than the jealousy of calf-love; even if he killed her it would not diminish her power over him.

The dominance of sexuality is further heightened by an affair in the school between two of the staff which is more or less witnessed by the boys. Sammy accepts that sex is the measure of all things and that the world is amoral and savage. He is already affected by the idea of justification by relative values. Hence if the world is savage immediate, though narrow, satisfactions are in order:

> The supply of nineteenth-century optimism and goodness had run out before it reached me. I transformed Nick's innocent, paper world. Mine was an amoral, a

> savage place in which man was trapped without hope . . . In my too susceptible mind sex dressed itself in gorgeous colours, brilliant and evil. I was in that glittering net, then, just as the silk moths were when they swerved and lashed their slim bodies and spurted the pink musk of their mating. Musk, shameful and heady, be thou my good.[7]

Just before he leaves school he gets the head's advice on life: you can always get what you want, provided you make a sacrifice for it.

His moment of decision, of choice after which he is no longer free of contingency but irrevocably committed to cause and effect, comes in an ecstatic experience on a hot summer evening. All nature seems to be sexually alive and Sammy begins by blissfully and innocently enjoying the sympathetic urges within him: but gradually he also associates Beatrice with his feelings and then associates the power of the will with sex in an effort to assert his control:

> . . . I said in the hot air what was important to me; namely the white, unseen body of Beatrice Ifor, her obedience, and for all time my protection of her; and for the pain she had caused me, her utter abjection this side death.[8]

In his mental turmoil he thinks to cool his hot and sticky body in a weir and senses that this invitation of the water is a sign from "the angel of the gate of paradise" to save him from succumbing to the flesh. But once in the water his body finds confirmation of its natural urges and the decision of all decisions is made:

> I stripped off and plunged in and I experienced my skin, from head to foot, firm smooth confinement of all my treasures. Now I knew the weight and shape of a man, his temperature, his darknesses. I knew myself

[7] *Op. cit.*, p. 226; pp. 231-2. [8] *Op. cit.*, pp. 235-6.

to shoot the glances of my eye, to stand firm, to sow my seed from the base of the strong spine . . . I sat there (on the hill-side) between the earth and the sky, between cloister and street. The waters had healed me and there was the taste of potatoes in my mouth.[9]

Sammy achieves self-knowledge but opts for sex as an instrument of the will for the subjection of Beatrice. The rule of self over another, made object, is the loss of innocence. It is at this point in the novel that the ambiguity of the title finally unfolds its meanings. Sammy is free to fall, to choose: but having made a wrong, because self-centred, choice he thereafter must call to his aid the logic of cause and effect and be dependent on events as relative to each other in order to justify his actions. In this he has diminished himself to become mechanical as matter, a tool for a job. He has abrogated his soul: like matter he is in free fall, apparently stable but in fact falling as all things fall relative to each other simultaneously in space.

The last phase of the novel is near in time to Sammy's decision to write his apologia. He faces the results of his moment of choice, the final sequence in a series stretching back seven years to the time of his desertion of Beatrice. She is an inmate of a mental home, stupefied, animal-like, incontinent, probably the result of her anxiety state caused in the first instance by Sammy's exploitation. Though it is possible she might have developed that way in any case Sammy nevertheless accepts his responsibility.

The novel ends with a review of Nick's and Miss Pringle's world. Nick is by nature innocent and uncomplicated. For him all is simple, only the physical world exists and there is no torture of the spirit. Miss Pringle, on the other hand, is similar to Sammy. She too had lost her freedom and thereafter was condemned to

[9] *Op. cit.*, p. 236.

torturing Sammy—teaching him Scripture while hating him because he was ward of the Rector whom she had wanted to marry. He classifies Miss Pringle and himself as the guilty. The innocent or the wicked live in one world quite simply but the guilty live in two worlds at once and torture each other. Sammy has come to understand this dichotomy and prepares to visit Miss Pringle to offer his forgiveness for the way she had affected his life. But Miss Pringle is blind to the problem and complacently cannot see her guilt; she has deceived herself completely. The world of body and spirit seem terribly separate to Sammy. The physical world exists and the spirit passes through it unacknowledged:

> All day long the trains run on rails. Eclipses are predictable. . . . The gorgeous dance is self-contained, then; does not need the music which in my mad moments I have heard. Nick's universe is real.
>
> All day long action is weighed in the balance and found not opportune nor fortunate or ill-advised, but good or evil. For this mode which we must call the spirit breathes through the universe and does not touch it; touches only the dark things, held prisoner, incommunicado, touches, judges, sentences and passes on.
>
> Her world was real, both worlds are real. There is no bridge.[10]

The final passage of the novel is something of a trick ending but rightly reminds the reader of the central experience of Sammy's self-torture in the cell. It puts Sammy's position and his responsibility to himself quite clearly. When he concludes that there is no bridge between the physical and spiritual worlds he is being pusillanimous. The last paragraphs of the novel refer to his emergence from the cell and his realisation that it was only a sort of broom-cupboard. The slimy object was a forgotten floor-cloth. He comes out dazed to meet

[10] *Op. cit.*, pp. 252-3.

his judge (the interrogator) but finds there is none. His case has been dropped; his interrogator was wrong to use the methods he did: "The Herr Doktor does not know about peoples." It was an error of administration. Sammy tormented himself and had his transfiguration by means of a small cupboard and a damp floor-cloth. But what he experienced was genuine all the same. There is no judge because we are our own judges and Sammy has been made tortuously to justify his past to himself. Without the experience he would have remained in a state of complete self-deception like Miss Pringle.

The commandant's broken English—"peoples"—Sammy could only have understood at the time as referring to himself. The result of his revelation, however, is to make him review and judge by means of hindsight all his past experience and the motives of those he knew. Without his revelation, indirectly attributable to Halde, he could not know, as he now knows, about himself and others, hence his puzzling over the commandant's plural for a singular as if it were the Sphinx's riddle.

Sammy's last words: "There is no bridge" are something of a falling short. He talks like the old Sammy who always found himself forced to take the easier course of "logical" conclusions. The new Sammy, after his revelation, is no longer entitled to. He has achieved the self-understanding he set out to achieve: but he implies—and Golding with him—that by its visionary and apocalyptic nature this truth cannot be adapted without compromise to ordinary living.

Golding has obviously attempted in *Free Fall* to rely less than in his earlier novels on a series of metaphors and images. In *Free Fall* there is only one really important image—the darkness—which is placed in the heart of the book. Everything else that he wishes to convey about Sammy is done by means of recreating a social setting and period or by emblematic characters. On the surface *Free Fall* appears to be, like *The Pyramid*, the most naturalistic of Golding's novels. Yet as with the preceding books the impact of the work is more in its poetic revelation of a search for self-knowledge than as a portrait of the main character. Golding succeeds more than adequately in his evocation of Rotten Row and of the classrooms and teaching methods of the schools in the twenties and thirties. But the schematic portraits of Beatrice and of the other subsidiary but important characters diminish the roundness needed for a full understanding of them. There is certainly a progression from the old Sammy to the new: nevertheless, Golding has sacrificed a fullscale portrait of Sammy and emphasised instead his mental state. He has revealed how Sammy seeks and finds a pattern of meaning in his life by means of the tool of self-awareness provided by his visionary experience. The power of the book seems to lie more in the very process of the search than in involvement with Sammy as a person. Yet this lack does little to diminish its force. The necessity of Sammy's desire to explain himself to himself is never in doubt. There is nothing tedious about Sammy's compulsive sincerity though to follow him is by no means easy. The objection that "an obsessed 'lover' is relevant only if he works out his problems in his own way without external influence"[11] represents both the obtuse criticism this novel has usually received as well as perhaps the impatience with the type of mind we are dealing with and Golding's presentation of it. The attempt to push the label "naturalist" on *Free Fall* is no doubt the explanation. Why write a "naturalistic" novel about a mystical crisis? It would be to stress the incidental at the expense of the whole. Naturalistic techniques are prominent in *Free Fall* but they are only a means to an end, only part of its structure and a secondary part at that. They exist because of the need to refer to the past and convey the feel

[11] F. Karl, *A Reader's Guide to the Contemporary English Novel*, London 1962, p. 259.

of life as it had been for Sammy. Their effect proves subservient to the concern with a metaphysical search as the opening words of the novel suggest and the later ecstatic writing confirms. It is clear that for all the apparent naturalism Golding's real interest is in the evocation of a generalised dilemma of innocence called upon to justify itself to itself in a corrupt world. Not for nothing is Sammy Mountjoy split into Samuel, called by the Lord, and the average pleasure-loving man. The problem for Sammy is stated in the opening paragraph of the novel where ecstasy is paralleled by the world of ordinary living. The visionary lives close to the shops and the local; he is still "a burning amateur" and the consequences of his search are not fully resolved. Can he combine his new vision with the ordinary traffic of existence? Sammy has become—such is the object of the exercise—fully conscious of this divergence, but it seems unlikely that he can live with his knowledge and bridge the gap between body and soul.

CHAPTER VI

MANOEUVRES OF SELF-DECEIVING: *THE SPIRE*

If one is to assume that the novels in the published sequence represent also the sequence of composition then it would seem that *The Spire* closes a phase of writing for Golding. It is the culminating point of the method employed in the preceding works. Like them its principal concern is with the use of character and situation to convey not just a moral but a poetic embodiment and intensification of certain human failings, the whole novel being a vehicle that permits the reader to re-experience the self-searching of the protagonist. This is particularly obvious in the case of Pincher and Sammy; this is the aim and also the outcome of Jocelin's case in *The Spire*.

The style of writing, both spare and very intense at the same time, is sustained uniformly to the end with almost no intervention from the author. We come to recognise that the feverish urgency—though the novel is narrated in the third person—is something running parallel to Jocelin's anxiousness to build and complete his spire. We also learn that the feeling of tension reflects something about Jocelin that he is trying to hide and in particular to hide from himself. The tone of the novel—the element in it most often adversely criticised—is in fact a correlative to Jocelin's self-deception. It reflects the way he has tended all along to see things and direct things only as he wanted to in terms of his obsession about the spire, blinding himself to the truth. In this climactic experience of his life the erection of the spire upwards counterpoints Jocelin's obligation to descend into himself and learn the truth about himself that he has conveniently buried there in the dark cellarage of his mind.

All the novels up to and including *The Spire* have the basic theme of self-understanding and all are planned on the progression towards this moment, from complete blindness to illumination. This is a fundamental note that sounds throughout Golding's novels and is perhaps a sign of his close study of Greek literature, particularly of tragedy. The interest lies in observing the character as he learns about himself and of all the novels *The Spire* demands to be approached first from Golding's angle of presentation. The convention of allowing the reader (or spectator in a tragedy) to be in a favoured position of knowledge is kept to its minimum requirement. The reader is scarcely allowed to be a yard ahead of Jocelin at any point. This inevitably makes for some difficulty and also unfortunately for some unnecessary obscurity.

From the moment we meet Jocelin, dean of the cathedral, with his secret vision to crown his church with a colossal spike four hundred feet high, we suspect ironic contradictions in his thoughts and actions. He is determined to go on, though reason is against him, and trust in God knowing the foundations of the church are inadequate for a spire. He holds the model of the cathedral in his hands and sees it as a man lying on his back with the spire "springing, projecting, bursting, erupting from the heart of the building". In one sense this is true but in another the reader already inches enough beyond Jocelin to see through the exaggerated language to the naïvety of his vision.

There are other touches in the opening chapter to suggest a complex personality working behind Jocelin's simple intention to build the spire. He overhears two deacons gossiping and denouncing someone for his spiritual pride. He does not suspect they are referring to him because his mind is closed to such a possibility. Jocelin has, then, a reputation for pigheadedness though he thinks himself a saint. Already disturbing facts are established about the organisation of the building project. Pangall, the lame cleaner of the cathedral, is humiliated and victimised by the builders. He knows they have already killed a man and suspects he will be the next. He suggests the lack of faith others have in Jocelin's spire, which is known as Jocelin's Folly. The unruly builders have a superstitious feeling it will fall. Jocelin has a marked distaste for sexual matters as his reaction to the letter from his aunt, mistress to a king, suggests. She has provided money for the spire and in return wishes to be buried in the cathedral. Jocelin pointedly ignores her.

Already Golding has sketched in behind Jocelin the suggestions of a certain disdain for all that is not spiritual and a determination to push ahead with his desires at all costs, against people, who are mere instruments in a grander purpose, and against reason. No doubt these details gain value by hindsight but they are enough to put the reader on his guard against Jocelin and to make him observe him critically.

A pattern is established in the opening chapter that is repeated in various forms throughout the novel. Golding alternates Jocelin's idealism with the two main reservations he has established in the first chapter. He contrasts Jocelin's determination to glorify God with his exploitation of people, and with his fear and avoidance of sex. The first major crisis involves Pangall's young wife, Goody, and Roger Mason, the master-builder. Jocelin happens to see them together and knows exactly what their exchanged glances mean. He experiences a great, even inordinate, revulsion which can only be assuaged in a tormenting sexual dream where spire, church, and body become involved together. Ignorant of his true feelings Jocelin sees the situation as something that can fit in with his vision. The fear that he might lose the master-builder and his men, who had threatened to abandon their task, subsides when he realises how Goody can be used to keep Roger there.

Sex can be a tool for his purpose but a terrible price has to be paid for it. Immediately after a scene where Jocelin reveals his vision to Roger and persuades him to go ahead with the work in spite of the poor foundations we are hurled into the contrasting episode of Pangall's torture at the hands of the builders and his humiliation as the model spire is paraded before him as a phallus. In the chaos Jocelin is nearly crushed but he sees enough to realise that Pangall is no more and that Goody and Roger are inexorably confronted.

Any interpretation of this scene must use evidence that occurs later in the story. Jocelin, deserted by the builders at midsummer, realises from the sight of the bonfires that the men have gone off to some pagan devil-worshipping. Only then does he see that they must have murdered—ritually murdered?—Pangall. Only then does he see how he had tried to keep out of his mind the memory of the viscous mistletoe berry sticking to his shoe in the crossways of the cathedral. The death of Pangall, and Goody's later pregnancy by Roger, and then her death in childbirth, are all very important as part of the toll exacted of Jocelin by his self-deception. Though the point about Jocelin's true motives does eventually become clear this whole episode and its later references are too obscure to make the impact they should except by dint of extra effort on the reader's part. It is an obscurity in the novel that has frequently been passed over.[1] Yet the results of it begin the process of breakdown that forces Jocelin into himself to face facts he had ignored. At Goody's death he realises how he had arranged the

[1] Comments on Pangall's death are only to be found in D. W. Crompton, "*T.S.*", *Critical Quarterly*, Spring, 1967; M. Kinkead-Weekes and I. Gregor, *William Golding. A critical study*, London 1967, p. 211; D. Roper, "Allegory and Novel in Golding's *T.S.*", *Wisconsin Studies in Contemporary Literature*, Winter 1967.

marriage with the impotent Pangall and had unwittingly helped to bring Goody and Roger together in the first instance. Even so he manoeuvres himself into a position of self-justification without realising the irony lurking in his thoughts:

> Yet like a birth itself, words came, that seemed to fit the totality of his life, his sins, and his forced cruelty, and above all the dreadful glow of his dedicated will. They were words that the choir boys sang sometimes at Easter . . .
> *This have I done for my true love.*[2]

The spire, however, still rises and with it Jocelin's hope that he is establishing the one good thing in a corrupt world, an ark, a refuge, a ship that he will fit with a mast. The pillars strain and bend but eventually settle down, the capstone is fitted and everything is ready at last, after two years, for the placing of the relic, a Holy Nail. This is brought from Rome by the Visitor, a sort of ecclesiastical inspector. There is a delay while an enquiry goes on into the running of the cathedral, the closing down of services, the use of church money. Jocelin openly admits his exploitation of people but still believes it was necessary:

> She (Goody) is woven into it everywhere. She died and then she came alive in my mind. She's there now . . . And I must have known about him before, you see, down in the vaults, the cellarage of my mind. But it was all necessary, of course. Like the money.[3]

Jocelin has no case that can please an orthodox inspector. A vision is something eccentric. He is forced to yield and is confined.

A great gale blows up and in his fear that the spire may fall Jocelin takes it on himself to uphold it with faith, with the Nail. He climbs to the top through wind and

[2] *T.S.*, p. 137. [3] *Op. cit.*, p. 166.

rain, battered by the elements, feeling them around him as devils he must defeat. When he has driven in the Nail he knows the spire will stand. In his exalted state he has a vision of Goody who seems to welcome him and resolve his tensions. He associates the achievement of the spire with his love for her. Still justifying himself Jocelin wrongly interprets even this glimpse of the truth as an atonement for the way he had manipulated her life.

If Jocelin has understood anything by this time it is only his sense of achievement; he has not understood his own humanity. By a careful reversal of the pattern whereby Jocelin has been in the ascendant, moving people around as objects in a game, Golding now prepares the last phase of the novel where Jocelin is revealed to himself as just as much an object to be manipulated as anyone else. A series of confrontations, face to face, finally convinces him of the way he has avoided the truth lying behind his motives and actions.

The first is with his aunt, the Lady Alison. Her presence throws his motives into relief. Jocelin thinks of himself as chosen by God and thereafter the appointed chooser of others, like Roger, as tools for God's work. Alison points out how it was she who did the choosing. Granted a favour as a mistress of the king she chose, half out of vengeance on her pious sister, to use her sexuality as a means of securing her nephew's preferment. Jocelin is only a part of a system of choosing, using, bartering, exploiting. He begins to see that he is used as he had used others. This first part of Jocelin's self-awareness, out of which he cannot manoeuvre, is then set in a wider and grander context. It is discovered that the bulging pillars, although they hold the strain, have subsided enough to put the spire out of the true and are in fact soft at the centre. They had been filled with rubble by the men of faith, "the giants who had been on earth in those days", who had built them. The angel that Jocelin thought was at his back warming him to his task was a devil leading him astray in a wilderness of corrupt values which Jocelin could not see for the blindness of his immediate purpose:

> Then all things came together. His spirit threw itself down an interior gulf, down, throw away, offer, destroy utterly, build me in with the rest of them; and as he did this he threw his physical body down too, knees, face, chest, smashing on the stone.
>
> Then his angel put away the two wings from the cloven hoof and struck him from arse to the head with a whitehot flail. It filled his spine with sick fire and he shrieked because he could not bear it yet knew he would have to.[4]

Jocelin can deceive himself no longer; the process of revelation continues. He turns to the record of his youthful vision that he had set down in a notebook. He begins to doubt the wisdom of his sacrifice. In thinking he was offering his all he was deceiving himself: "When I threw myself down and offered myself to the work, I thought that to offer myself was the same as to offer everything. It was my stupidity."

Jocelin's second confrontation is with Father Anselm, his confessor, who denounces the way Jocelin's preferment had come so easily to him when he was only a minimal priest, unworthy of his office. Jocelin realises the need to atone for his guilt. He seeks out Roger, now reduced to drink and professionally finished, to seek his forgiveness. In this third confrontation he at last faces the truth. He admits that though he thought he was doing great work he was only breeding hate. He sees his sanctity as bogus and himself as a fool and a guilty man—"a building with a vast cellarage where the rats live".

He receives Roger's forgiveness in a convulsive embrace of unbridled emotion but when it has subsided the whole truth is still not laid bare. Since the building still

[4] *Op. cit.*, p. 188.

stands perhaps they were necessary to each other, visionary and mason, as instruments of a grander scheme. In a final manoeuvre to avoid facing the real source of his motives and exonerate himself Jocelin taunts Roger with his share in the spire and, without really wishing to, is impelled by his devil to suggest Roger atone for Pangall's death by suicide—"poor Pangall, crouched beneath the crossways, with a sliver of mistletoe between his ribs". But even as he says it Jocelin is over the crisis and knows himself fully at last—he had wanted Goody for himself: "What's a man's mind Roger? Is it the whole building, cellarage and all? . . . The trouble is that the cellarage knew about him—knew he was impotent I mean—and arranged the marriage."

Driven out in anger by Roger he collapses. The final chapter concerns the review of Jocelin's motives and his opinion of the human condition as he lies in semi-consciousness before death, in "some new kind of life", where his thoughts seem to last a century or a second. As his mind returns to the cellarage and its contents he half hears how Roger has tried to hang himself and failed. The full meaning of humanity begins to come over him—people must be treated as people, not objects: "If I could go back, I would take God as lying between people and to be found there." Goody herself was only an unattainable sexual object and his spire points for ever to Berenice's hair in the sky. People are committed, in the process of living, to exploiting each other and there is no source of appeal outside themselves: "There is no innocent work. God knows where God may be." As the priest gives him absolution to help him into heaven Jocelin realises that heaven is nowhere unless he can clear himself with the people he has used, Roger and Goody, and go there hand in hand with them. He realises his error: "I traded a stone hammer for four people", for Roger's wife, Rachel and Pangall were part of his scheme too. Jocelin's final thought, as his sight clears enough for him to see the spire through the window, unites the amazing achievement with its confused and questionable origins. It rushes "upward to some point at the sky's end, and with a silent cry. It was slim as a girl, translucent."

It reminds him of his delight in seeing an appletree in flower and his thoughts at the time that there were roots and branches to the tree besides the glorious flowers. The glory cannot exist without the rest. Jocelin unites at the moment of extinction the two impulses of his life—the urge towards glory and a disregard of the sordid roots. The spire as a symbol of achievement survives and despite the motives behind its origin it is a beautiful thing "like the appletree".

The ending of *The Spire* is fine and unequivocal. Jocelin is stripped down to honesty, happy to shed his self-deception: but he realises how lonely a being he has become by creating his own isolation. The spire is beautiful, but compromised like life. Frequently in the latter part of the novel life is compared to a rickety building. In this, the most poetic statement in his novels, Golding evokes—and the force of his work prevents it from being an arid analogy—the interplay between light and dark in life, the soaring spire and the cellarage. The perfection of goodness cannot exist on its own. The spire must go down as far as it goes up is an engineering rule of thumb mentioned early in the story and for Jocelin this has meant the descent into the cellarage. The spire survives but with the same perilous balance as our human intercourse.

The Spire is the finest symbolic expression of Golding's intention to make people understand their own humanity yet it has been attacked for implausibility and obscurity through and through. To recall the instance of Salisbury spire itself—no doubt the model for Jocelin's—over four hundred feet high and nearly two feet out of the perpendicular is enough to dispel the impossibility of such a spire surviving upon inadequate foundations. More serious are the objections to character portrayal and the presentation of events in the novel. It is true the subsidiary characters remain very shadowy and lend themselves too easily to the author's purpose, though in fairness one must point out, since the novel is projected through the personality of Jocelin, that we generally see the subsidiary characters in the purblind way Jocelin does. Jocelin is not meant to be very perceptive. The objections that have been made to Jocelin can be summed up by the view that "illusion is proclaimed but not created".[5] However this is to go excessively against Golding especially since he has built into Jocelin's character numerous instances where Jocelin betrays his thoughts without knowing it. He also implies an ironic view of Jocelin's judges who are a pair of gossiping deacons, an envious confessor, and a whore who has lived for the gratification of her desires and little else. Their self-deception enriches his basic theme without being heavy handed.

In fact the objections to *The Spire* lie more in the question of subtlety and compression than anything else. Certainly the quality of writing gains by it. The impression of building a medieval cathedral and the agony of Jocelin on his deathbed come over particularly well. The price of compression is not so much in character portrayal as in the danger of foxing the reader. On the question of Pangall and Goody there is the undeniable fact that the reader is being made to work too hard and the resulting confusion might easily lead some to abandon the task.

This would indeed be unfortunate especially if it were to discourage the reading of all five novels in sequence. They have common ground between them and present a similar imaginative experience in spite of their im-

[5] V. S. Pritchett, "God's Folly", *New Statesman*, 10 Apr. 1964, p. 562.

pressive technical diversity. In particular the novels share the twin themes of darkness in the heart of man and the idea that there is a "grace" or salvation to be found in our becoming aware of our condition. Of all the characters Jocelin comes nearest, as a grown man, to looking the darkness in the face though he has avoided it long enough by various manoeuvres. True, he is a victim of the cellarage but he is also its victor. Golding allows Jocelin his victorious self-awareness but he exists in an age removed from our own and his self-knowledge coincides with his death. That self-deception diminishes our humanity is proven beyond doubt and also imaginatively projected. The part of the problem that Golding does not examine in these novels is how one is to behave when the state of self-awareness has been achieved. Yet the implications of his point of view and the relevance of these novels, whatever their setting or period, is clearly to the present. What counts is to understand *now*, perfection *now*. For Pincher it was too late, perhaps even for Sammy. For Jocelin it is worked out in time though confined to his final moments of life. It seems Golding is holding out to the reader a bitterly impossible and tormenting choice: perfection cannot exist *now*, yet it must exist *now*.

Golding's "solution" is a compassionate understanding, the quality a truly great artist cannot be without. He is a visionary writer seeking to find the balance between body and soul. The mere life of the body, like Pincher's is only half the story. To be only a Mouth is not to be fully human. The denial of the body on the other hand and the escape into false spiritual adventures such as Jocelin lives by are equally a lie. The only solution for these errors is the realisation of them, facing up to them, though accepting at the same time that victory over them is rare and exceptional. Golding's conclusion would thus appear to be not a bitter one but a compassionate one.

On the question of the split between body and soul,

the imperfection resulting from it and the need to close the gap or at least soothe it Golding seems to share ground with another visionary poet: Traherne. In his *Third Century of Meditations* he deals with the idea of a falling off, a corruption and the need to come to terms with this essentially human dilemma:

> Eternity was manifest in the light of the day, and something infinite behind everything appeared, which talked with my expectation and moved my desire . . . The skies were mine, and so were the sun and moon and stars, and all the world was mine, and I the only spectator and enjoyer of it. I knew no churlish proprieties, nor bounds, nor divisions; but all proprieties and divisions were mine: all treasures and the possessors of them. So that with much ado I was corrupted; and made to learn the dirty devices of this world. Which now I unlearn, and become as it were a little child again, that I may enter into the Kingdom of God.

Golding it seems stops at ". . . I was corrupted; and made to learn the dirty devices of this world". He indicates, notably by means of Simon and Jocelin, the furthest point of human understanding but feels obliged also to remove them from the human scene. He implies that innocence and perfection are incompatible with the human condition but he implies equally that the urge and compulsion to strive after them is our tragic fate.

CHAPTER VII

COMIC AND TRAGI-COMIC

There is a side to Golding which his first five novels, because of their powerful impact, have tended to obscure. He has an inclination to a mildly satiric style which he has indulged in his *nouvelle*, *Envoy Extraordinary* (1956), and its stage-adaptation, *The Brass Butterfly* (1958). In its story form we encounter the basic situation and ideas. Phanocles, the inventor, arrives with the veiled but unbelievably beautiful Euphrosyne at the court of one of the Roman Emperors. He wishes to present his inventions and seek a patron for them so that he can change the world and make machines do the slave-work. He is immediately countered by the Emperor's view that Progress is almost always for the worst. Phanocles has three toys for Caesar; the first two are a pressure-cooker and explosives to fire a projectile. Only the pressure-cooker appeals to Caesar and Phanocles is tolerated on that account. The inventor, however, has more interest in the model ship he has brought for steam can convert her into a warship. He is allowed to apply his pressure-cooker principle to an old barge and adapt her as a warship, the *Amphitrite*. In the confusion of the appearance of Postumus, the Heir Designate, who had suspected the Emperor of having armed himself with secret weapons for some sinister purpose, the *Amphitrite* goes berserk and sinks. She has been fired by slaves who fear redundancy. There is still the projectile and Postumus rushes off to commandeer it. It backfires and kills him, the result of the removal of the safety device, the brass butterfly, by a thoughtful Euphrosyne. The apparently foolish Emperor is wiser than the clever inventor. He sees through Phanocles' motives for keeping Euphrosyne veiled. She has a harelip, a flaw in her beauty that would have prevented anyone taking any interest in her and perhaps in Phanocles and his inventions as well. She has been a tool for Phanocles but the Emperor offers generously to marry her—only nominally at his age—and preserve her secret. He is delighted with the pressure-cooker and its gastronomic magic "the most Promethean discovery of them all", but explains to Phanocles where the danger lies. He places inventions before people. He is infatuated with such a narrow view of his inventions that he cannot see how people are to him "an interruption, an intrusion". However, since the Emperor is impressed with the civilising influence of the pressure-cooker Phanocles is eager to bring out his third invention—printing. The Emperor is delighted until he thinks of the interesting biographies it will breed, the memoirs, the scholarly disquisitions, the mountains of unreadable statistics. There is only one solution: make Phanocles an ambassador and pack him off, with his gunpowder and printing, to China.

In the stage-version the outline remains but the changes necessarily introduced tend to broaden the wittier parts of the story to the point of obviousness and the dialogue, even when keeping closely to the story, takes on an unfortunate archness. There is a problem of theatrical projection over and above the question of content that Golding, rather surprisingly considering his experience as an actor, has not fully resolved.

The Brass Butterfly is a play that is bound to appear satisfactory rather than particularly good. The general view of it in performance was that it provided a good vehicle for Alastair Sim (the Emperor), but was otherwise not substantial enough. The changes and adaptations bear this out. The romantic interest provided by Euphrosyne and the Emperor's grandson is expanded and she is given a motive for stealing the safety device in being a Christian: but everything that touches these characters seems jejune. Phanocles is made to push his argument about Progress a little too hard and the Emperor appears so garrulous that he loses the civilised hauteur of the Emperor in the story-version. It is the Emperor nevertheless who is the most successfully created character in the play and he has the best lines. Golding has some good fun with the anachronisms but it is only good fun; the satire is a mild purgative. He admits as much in his Introduction to the school edition of the play but at the same time wants us to take Phanocles very seriously indeed:

> Day by day he continues to exercise his partial foresight, at once rapt by the fascination of the game, and indifferent to the end result of it. He is indeed, a force of nature. He is the power of man himself. There is no stopping him; for this is our tragic condition. We must invent and change, we must control and let loose; if we stop, we shall die out like the dinosaurs.[1]

This comes very near to one of Golding's main themes in his novels but its effect in the play is certainly to be applauded more in the intention than in the realisation. Golding claims in connexion with his novels to make the reader see things his way. In *The Brass Butterfly* this is what fails to come over and explains its flatness. The "public" form of a play seems, to judge from this example, to inhibit the originality of his talent. Moreover, the comic is not a style in which, so far at least, Golding is at his most telling. It is as if he is using the part of his range where his voice is adequate rather than effective.

The best tone for him seems to be more the tragicomic than the comic and this he shows to considerable advantage in his most recent novel, *The Pyramid*. As one might expect styles do not begin and end in fixed places

[1] *B.B.*, p. 4.

and in Golding's case the tendency to use the tragi-comic tone exists in his work as far back as *Free Fall* (1959). Already in that novel the portrait of Sammy's lonely queer guardian, the Rector, Father Watts-Watt, is both grotesque and moving. The tiny tentative advances he makes to Sammy contrast with the enormous desire for love that his non-life has succeeded in thwarting.[2] A similar blend of the comic and the ridiculous forms the basis of his portrait of Miss Pulkinhorn in the short-story of that name on the theme of the biter bit (1960). She is a predatory bigot who spies on an ecstatic almost lunatic man who comes to pray at *her* cathedral. The narrator, the organist, tells of a little contretemps where she gets locked in the cathedral all night after witnessing the man's final ecstasy and fears a scandal by association. They play a little game with each other for some time pretending the incident didn't happen until one day the organist finds her praying in the chapel the man had always used. Her vigorous hate seems to have led first to emulation and then contrite reversal.

This particular blend of the grotesque and the saddening appears to be the newest development in Golding's style. It is given full prominence in *The Pyramid* and reflects the desire for change that he feels is essential to a writer.[3] The new approach has its roots in *Free Fall* where Sammy's crisis is placed in a social setting, but now the emphasis is more firmly on explaining events and people by reference to behaviour and motivation. The protagonist, Oliver, experiences normal feelings rather soberly; there are no complex spiritual crises like those of Pincher, Sammy or Jocelin. The three parts that make up the novel are three separate stories which are, on the level of events, only tenuously connected. There are several themes, however, that bind

[2] See particularly *F.F.*, pp. 162-4.

[3] See B. Dick, "The Novelist is a Displaced Person", *College English*, Mar. 1965, p. 481.

them more closely together and also a narrator, Oliver, whom we meet at two critical points in his adolescence and then finally in the third story as a mature man. The symbol of the pyramid itself is far more subtly placed behind the book than similar poetic devices in the earlier works. Only gradually with the conclusion of the novel does its effect impose itself on the reader for then one of the most important themes emerges clearly. Oliver has matured to the apex of a pyramid but at the same time that emotional development has meant a climb and a climb using other people as steps in a progression. There are suggestions too that the pyramid represents the social hierarchy of the stodgy little town of Stilbourne, but this part of the symbol has very little to communicate since Golding is not particularly convincing or subtle in conveying the class differences of the thirties. When the novel, in its last section, emerges into the sixties the alleged changes have to be taken for granted rather than as something that has been felt to happen or exist in the novel. *The Pyramid* was clearly intended in part to deal more than any of Golding's previous novels with the interplay of social relationships. Yet its strength lies elsewhere.

The epigraph to the novel suggests the breadth of interpretation Golding wants the reader to maintain—"If thou be among people make for thyself love, the beginning and end of the heart"—and finally he no doubt carries the reader with him. But the presentation of this basic theme is narrowly restricted to love in the sense of sexuality, whether perverted to excess or repressed to excess, which is in both cases self-destructive. The first story centres on Oliver and Evie in late adolescence and moves from farcical comedy to sadness as we follow Oliver's plans to have sex with Evie at all costs. Evie is already very promiscuous, the result of the sadistically brutal, almost incestuous, passion of her father. While Oliver is scheming to have her she is planning to seduce him on an exposed escarpment in full view of his father. For Oliver, when he confronts his father, the realisation of what he has done is the end of innocence. When he meets Evie again a few years later their conversation reveals her masochistic dependence on sex and she accuses Oliver of rape, putting the responsibility for her already existing nymphomania on him. At first he doesn't understand but gradually he begins to see her as a person who had her own problems though at first she had appeared as an object to be pursued and used.

In the second story concerning Oliver and the Stilbourne Operatic Society the tone of comic exaggeration is maintained to the end. Oliver, now an undergraduate devoted to science, meets Mr de Tracy, the exaggerated camp guest producer. In an exchange of views about the meaning of existence Oliver can only speak in his limited callow way. To him "It's like chemistry. You can take it as a *thing*—or you can take it as a *thing*." This impasse represents Oliver's dilemma over the assertion of the self. He cannot at the moment see beyond the necessity to develop by using people about him as things. This is what Mr de Tracy explains to him obliquely by showing him what the truth is in his own case. He produces photographs that show him dressed as a ballerina. The self will find a means of assertion; it can do nothing else even if it takes a queer turn.

The tone of the second story even in Mr de Tracy's revelation preserves a kind of whimsicality which makes for an interlude between the darker parts of the book. The third story is a blend of the grotesque and the tragic. This is concerned with Bounce, Oliver's music teacher, a spinster so dominated by her father's harshness that she becomes ungracious and mannish. For all her music she is spiritually dead. She is the creation of the sadistic teaching of a cold and unsympatnetic father who has an eye for the absolute rather than people. She is taken up and looked after by Henry Williams who starts from nothing as a chauffeur in the thirties to arrive in the sixties as a prosperous garage owner. This he does by way of enlightened self-interest, using Bounce's money and property. It is perhaps more a case of symbiosis than exploitation pure and simple. But to others, notably Oliver's mother, Henry is a wily Welshman with a flair for business. Bounce too senses she is being used and this feeling emerges in a way that reveals her mental disturbance. She begins to do almost anything for affection and attention—abandoning her car so that Henry has to come for her, driving dangerously, and finally walking nude in the street.

The story is told as part of a return journey to Stilbourne by Oliver, now a mature man and a father, as he stands before her grave. He is aware that Bounce had contracted out of life; as a woman she was not fulfilled, her body was unused. (She contrasts with Evie who could be said to have used it wrongly or too much.) Oliver rejects all that non-life of Bounce's and realises at last as he takes leave of the prosperous Henry that the lesson of life is a wary compromise. Pay one must but no more than a reasonable price.

To some extent this tragi-comic view is also a commonsense view and balances the unrelenting all-or-nothing tragic tone of the first five novels. It is possible to argue that in pitching his tone lower Golding has produced a novel more like life and experience such as they are commonly known, but has forfeited the intense style of his earlier work and thereby something of his grip on the reader. If this is so it would apply more to the first two parts of the novel than the last where he regains the richness of suggestion of his earlier work while realising the character of Bounce as fully credible and moving.

Golding's literary career has been brief—only about twelve years so far—but also very concentrated and has remained even in quality almost entirely throughout his range. He has travelled an enormous distance since *Lord of the Flies* in 1954 and his career seems particularly remarkable when one remembers that it almost never started at all; it is alleged that *Lord of the Flies* was rejected by twenty-one publishers.[4] Yet without *Lord of the Flies* Golding could never have made the conquest he has made as one of the finest of post-war British novelists. It has the important quality of accessibility allied to Golding's intransigence in his point of view. Had his career begun with, say, *Pincher Martin* or *The Inheritors*, it is likely that the technical difficulties alone would have kept readers at bay. However, his popular reputation was made by *Lord of the Flies* and to judge from the work published so far this is likely to remain so for part of the quality of Golding's imagination is the relentless pursuit of a point of view with no concession to easy reading. This could so easily lead him away from contemporary life into a world of private obsessions. Yet it has never done so and here lies part of the secret of his hold on modern readers. It is not necessary, in his view, for a writer to be "engaged" in order to be modern; current affairs are only incidental. The writer's real job is to show man *sub specie aeternitatis*:

> The distinction between them (current affairs) and the general human background is vague; felt by the novelist rather than defined. But what is apparent to him—dare one say 'to him rather than to most'?—is that current affairs are only expressions of the basic human condition where his true business lies. If he has a serious, an Aeschylean, preoccupation with the human tragedy, that is only to say that he is committed to looking for the root of the disease instead of describing the symptoms. I can't help feeling that critics of this Aeschylean outlook are those who think they have an

[4] J. R. Baker, *William Golding. A Critical Study*, New York 1965, p. xv.

> easy answer to all problems simply because they have never looked further than the rash appearing on the skin.[5]

This preoccupation is at its most evident in *Lord of the Flies*. In spite of the distance of the subject feelings deep within us that have been made raw by recent historical events come to the surface, and plausible parallels are never far away from the words on the page. Of all the novels this is the one closest to a contemporary historical explanation—although that is only a limited interpretation—and hence easiest to get to grips with. Yet this connexion is only incidental to a more universal examination of human nature and what Golding has gone on to do from there is less easy to place. The inhumanity of war has simply prompted him to go deeper into the emergence of our sense of guilt, into an area of personal dilemmas which is, by the nature of his enquiry, not easy for most readers to penetrate. He has also become, in a certain sense, even more grim if one considers how absent from his world are happy expressions of love and generosity. Yet it is not the grimness of cynicism but rather of dogged understanding. In his outlook Golding must be considered by the weight of his work a philosophical and religious novelist but not in the sense of being "churchy" nor in the sense of an original thinker illustrating a system. This, however, would be nothing without his considerable literary gifts and his poetic force. Even the adverse criticism Golding has received has always acknowledged the power of his imagination and the technical brilliance.

Yet for all the technique the reader cannot escape the content of Golding's work. It is impossible, during the reading of a Golding novel, to separate the aesthetic pleasure in the writing from the moral impact of the

[5] Contribution to "The Writer in his Age," *London Magazine*, May 1957, p. 45.

author's point of view even when one disagrees with it. He has, at his best, a poetic mesmerising force that must surely prove time-resisting. The effect is that no reader can come away from his work other than in the way the author wants him to—shaken. Clearly Golding intends that his work should primarily disturb.

The human condition for Golding implies, in the first instance, the necessary subjection of other human beings but also brings with it the saving grace of our being able to meditate on this inherent tendency that seeks to deny our humanity, contemplate it and ideally overcome it. The tragic in the human condition is that the battle is endless except for an élite and even they, Golding implies—his Simons and Jocelins—are victors in one sense only to be victims in another. There is a most important ethical point involved by implication in the world of Golding's novels—a point conveyed of course obliquely and feelingly, not aridly and explicitly stated. It is that man becomes aware of his own nature and also of what is right and wrong at the same time. In the past Golding has always conveyed this by means of dramatic and poetic means—the hyperbole of an emotional crisis: Simon and the Beast, Tuami's realisation of good and evil, Pincher's self-creation and destruction, Sammy's and Jocelin's ecstasy. In *The Pyramid* he appears to move from the tragic to a tragi-comic realisation of the self. By implication Oliver's self-awareness is a life-long and slow process rather than a momentary illumination. The tragi-comic may well be the style best suited in future for conveying the dichotomy Golding senses in the human condition and for relating it to normal experience. The instinct to know ourselves, which is the prime fact of our humanity, and the instinct blindly to assert our destructive will in using other people need not be exclusive of each other but can—must—be understood, accepted, and blended together.

BIBLIOGRAPHY

References in the text, where more than one edition is concerned, are marked * in this Bibliography.

I am indebted to the studies by J. R. Baker and by B. S. Oldsey and S. Weintraub for some of the entries concerning American publications.

I. WORKS BY WILLIAM GOLDING

1. *Poems*

Poems. London and Toronto (Macmillan) 1934; New York 1935. In "Macmillan's Contemporary Poets", 34 pp.

2. *Novels*

Lord of The Flies. London (Faber) 1954. New York (Coward-McCann) 1955. London (Faber paper covered edn.) 1958. New York (Putnam Capricorn paperback edn.) 1959 with commentary by E. L. Epstein. Harmondsworth (Penguin) 1960, in "Penguin Modern Classics". New York (Coward-McCann) 1962 with an introduction by E. M. Forster. London (Faber) 1962, school edn. with introduction and notes by Ian Gregor and Mark Kinkead-Weekes. *London (Faber papercovered edn.) 1962, illustrated with stills from the film by Peter Brook, 4 plates. New York (Odyssey Press) 1963.

The Inheritors. London (Faber) 1955. *London (Faber paper covered edn.) 1961. New York (Harcourt, Brace & World) 1962; paperback 1963. London (Faber) 1964, school edn. with introduction and notes by Ian Gregor and Mark Kinkead-Weekes.

Pincher Martin. London (Faber) 1956. New York (Harcourt, Brace & World) 1957 under the title: *The Two Deaths of Christopher Martin*. *London (Faber paper covered edn.) 1960. Harmondsworth (Penguin) 1962.

Free Fall. London (Faber) 1959. New York (Harcourt, Brace & World) 1960; paperback 1962. *London (Faber paper covered edn.) 1961. Harmondsworth (Penguin) 1963.

The Spire. London (Faber) 1964. New York (Harcourt, Brace & World) 1964. *London (Faber paper covered edn.) 1965.

The Pyramid. London (Faber) 1967.

3. *Drama*

The Brass Butterfly: Play in 3 acts. London (Faber) 1958. New York (New American Library) 1962. *London (Faber) 1963, school edn. with an introduction by the author.

4. *Miscellaneous*

"Envoy Extraordinary" in *Sometime, Never—Three Tales of Imagination.* *London (Eyre & Spottiswoode) 1956. New York (Ballantine) 1956; paperback 1962.

"Miss Pulkinhorn", short story, in *Encounter*, Aug. 1960. pp. 27-32.

Break My Heart, BBC Radio Feature, 1962, Unpublished.

"On the escarpment" (Part I of *The Pyramid*) in *Kenyon Review*, June 1967.

5. *Essays and Articles*

Several of the following have been reprinted in *The Hot Gates and other occasional pieces*, London (Faber), 1965, and are marked by a † below.

"The Writer in his Age", in *London Magazine*, May 1957.

"Pincher Martin", in *Radio Times*, 21 Mar. 1958.

†"The Ladder and the Tree", in *The Listener*, 24 Mar. 1960.

"In Retreat", in *Spectator*, 25 Mar. 1960.

"Raider", in *Spectator*, 20 May 1960.

†"Islands", in *Spectator*, 10 Jun. 1960.

†"On the Crest of the Wave", in *Times Literary Supplement*, 17 Jun. 1960; reprinted in *The Writer's Dilemma*, Oxford University Press 1961.

†"Headmasters", in *Spectator*, 12 Aug. 1960.

†"In my Ark", in *Spectator*, 16 Sep. 1960.

"Man of God", in *Spectator*, 7 Oct. 1960.

†"Billy the Kid", in *Spectator*, 25 Nov. 1960.

"Prospect of Eton", in *Spectator*, 25 Nov. 1960.

"Thin Partitions", in *Spectator*, 13 Jan. 1961.

"Rise of Love", in *Spectator*, 10 Feb. 1961.

"Androids All", in *Spectator*, 24 Feb. 1961.

"All or Nothing", in *Spectator*, 24 Mar. 1961.

"Before the Beginning", in *Spectator*, 26 May 1961.

†"Astronaut by Gaslight", in *Spectator*, 9 Jun. 1961.

"It's a long way to Oxyrhynchus", in *Spectator*, 7 Jul. 1961.

"Party of One: Thinking as a Hobby", in *Holiday Magazine*, Aug. 1961.

†"Tolstoy's Mountain", in *Spectator*, 8 Sep. 1961.

†"Touch of Insomnia", in *Spectator*, 27 Oct. 1961.

†"English Channel", in *Holiday Magazine*, Nov. 1961.

†"Glass Door", in *Spectator*, 24 Nov. 1961.
"Through the Dutch Waterways", in *Holiday Magazine*, Jan. 1962.
†"Body and Soul", in *Spectator*, 19 Jan. 1962.
†"Shakespeare's Birthplace", in *Holiday Magazine*, May 1962.
†"Gradus ad Parnassum", in *Spectator*, 7 Sep. 1962.
"Surge and Thunder", in *Spectator*, 14 Sep. 1962.
†"Digging for Pictures", in *Holiday Magazine*, Mar. 1963.

II. CRITICISM

1. *Works on Golding*

BAKER, J. R.: *William Golding*, New York (St Martin's Press) 1965.
HYNES, SAMUEL: *William Golding*, New York and London (Columbia University Press) 1964, in Columbia Essays on Modern Writers.
KINKEAD-WEEKES, MARK AND GREGOR, IAN: *William Golding. A Critical Study*, London (Faber) 1967.
MOODY, PHILIPPA: *A Critical Commentary on William Golding's "Lord of the Flies"*, London (Macmillan) 1966.
OLDSEY, BERNARD S. AND WEINTRAUB, STANLEY: *The Art of William Golding*, New York (Harcourt, Brace & World) 1965.

2. *General Studies with chapters or pages devoted to Golding*

ALLEN, WALTER: *Tradition and Dream* (Pelican), Harmondsworth (Penguin) 1965.
AMIS, KINGSLEY: *New Maps of Hell*, London (Gollancz) 1961.
BROES, ARTHUR T.: *Lectures on Modern Novelists*, Pittsburgh, Pa. (Carnegie Series in English, No. 7) 1963.
BURGESS, ANTHONY: *The Novel Today*, London (Longmans) 1963.
——: *The Novel Now*, London (Faber) 1967.
COX, C. B.: *The Free Spirit* London (Oxford University Press) 1963.
GINDIN, JAMES: *Post-War British Fiction*, London (Cambridge University Press) 1962.
KARL, FREDERICK: *A Reader's Guide to the Contemporary English Novel*, London (Thames & Hudson) 1963.
KERMODE, FRANK: *Puzzles and Epiphanies*, London (Routledge) 1962.
NELSON, WILLIAM (ed.): *William Golding's "Lord of the Flies". A Source Book*, New York (Odyssey Press) 1963.
WEST, PAUL: *The Modern Novel*, London (Hutchinson) 1963.

3. *Articles on Golding*

A number of articles concerning *Lord of the Flies* have been collected and edited by William Nelson (see above). They are marked (N) in the following list to indicate their availability in single volume form.

ALDRIDGE, JOHN W.: "William Golding", in *New York Times Book Review*, 10 Dec. 1961.
ALLEN, WALTER: "New Novels", in *New Statesman*, 25 Sep. 1954. (N)
AMIS, KINGSLEY: "A Man on Rockall", in *Spectator*, 9 Nov. 1956.
ANON.: "The cost of a vision", in *Times Literary Supplement*, 16 Apr. 1964.
——: "Down to earth", in *Times Literary Supplement*, 1 Jun. 1967.
BABB, HOWARD: "On the ending of *Pincher Martin*", in *Essays in Criticism*, Jan. 1964.
BLAKE, IAN: "*Pincher Martin*: William Golding and "Taffrail", in *Notes & Queries*, Aug. 1962.
BOWEN, JOHN: "One man's meat; the idea of individual responsibility", in *Times Literary Supplement*, 7 Aug. 1959. (N)
——: "Bending over backwards", in *Times Literary Supplement*, 23 Oct. 1959 (N)
BYATT, A. S.: "Of things I sing", in *New Statesman*, 2 Jun. 1967.
CAMPBELL, ARCHIE: "William Golding: *Pincher Martin*", in *From the Fifties* (BBC Radio Drama Series), eds. Michael Bakewell and Eric Evans, London 1961.
COHN, A. M.: "The Berengaria Allusion in *Lord of the Flies*", in *Notes & Queries*, Nov. 1966.
COLBY, V.: "William Golding", in *Wilson Library Bulletin*, vol. 37, Feb. 1963. (N)
COX, C. B.: "Lord of the Flies", in *Critical Quarterly*, Summer 1960. (N)
——: "William Golding's Pincher Martin", in *The Listener*, 12 Mar. 1964.
CROMPTON, D. W.: "The Spire", in *Critical Quarterly*, Spring 1967.
DAVIS, D. M.: "Golding, the Optimist, belies his Somber Pictures and Fiction", *National Observer*, 17 Sep. 1962.
——: "Conversation with Golding", in *New Republic*, 4 May 1963.
DICK, BERNARD: "The Novelist is a Displaced Person. An interview with William Golding", in *College English*, Mar. 1965.
DREW, PHILIP: "Second Reading", in *Cambridge Review*, 27 Oct. 1956. (N)
DREW, PHILIP: "Man on a cold wet rock", in *Cambridge Review*, 4 May 1957.
EGAN, JOHN, M.: "Golding's view of Man", in *America*, 26 Jan. 1963. (N)
FREEDMAN, RALPH: "The New Realism: the Fancy of William Golding", in *Perspective*, Summer-Autumn 1958. (N)
FULLER, EDMUND: "The Compelling Lure of William Golding. Behind the Vogue, a Rigorous Understanding", in *New York Herald Tribune Books*, 4 Nov. 1962. (N)

FURBANK, P. N.: "Golding's Spire", in *Encounter*, May 1964.
GALLAGHER, W. P.: "The human image in William Golding", in *Studies*, Summer-Autumn 1965.
GINDIN, JAMES: "Gimmick and Metaphor in the novels of William Golding", in *Modern Fiction Studies*, Summer 1960. (N) Reprinted in *Post-War British Fiction*, London 1962.
GRANDE, LUKE M.: "The Appeal of Golding", in *Commonweal*, 25 Jan. 1963. (N)
GREEN, MARTIN: "Distaste for the contemporary", in *The Nation*, 21 May 1960. (N)
GREEN, PETER: "The world of William Golding", in *A Review of English Literature*, Apr. 1960.
——: "The world of William Golding", *Transactions and Proceedings of the Royal Society of Literature*, vol. xxxii 1963. (N) Expanded form of the article in *A Review of English Literature*. See above.
GREGOR, IAN: "Aspiring", in *Manchester Guardian Weekly*, 16 Apr. 1964.
GREGOR, IAN AND KINKEAD-WEEKES, MARK: "The strange case of Mr Golding and his critics", in *Twentieth Century*, Feb. 1960 (N)
HAINSWORTH, J. D.: "William Golding", in *Hibbert Journal*, Summer 1966.
HALLE, L. J.: "Small Savages", in *Saturday Review*, 15 Oct. 1955. (N)
HAMPTON, T.: "An error in *Lord of the Flies*", in *Notes & Queries* Jul. 1965.
HARVEY, W. J.: "The reviewing of contemporary fiction", in *Essays in Criticism*, Apr. 1958.
HEBERT, HUGH: "Lord of the Tenace", in *Guardian*, 14 Jul. 1967.
HERNDL, G. C.: "Golding and Salinger: a clear choice", in *Wiseman Review*, Winter 1964-5.
HEWITT, D.: "New Novels", in *Manchester Guardian*, 28 Sep. 1954. (N)
HYNES, SAMUEL: "Novels of a Religious Man", in *Commonweal*, 18 Mar. 1960. (N)
KEARNS, F. E.: "Salinger and Golding: conflict on the campus", in *America*, 26 Jan. 1963. (N)
——: "Golding revisited", in *William Golding's "Lord of the Flies". A source book*, (ed.) William Nelson. See above.
KEARNS, F. E AND GRANDE, L. M.: "An exchange of views—'The Appeal of Golding' ", in *Commonweal*, 22 Feb. 1963 (N)
KERMODE, FRANK: "Coral islands", in *Spectator*, 22 Aug. 1958. (N)
——: Interview with Golding. BBC Third Programme, 28 Aug. 1959. Published in *Books and Bookmen*, 5 Oct. 1959.
——: "Free Fall", in *Spectator*, 23 Oct. 1959.

——: "The novels of William Golding", in *International Literary Annual* vol. iii, 1961. (N) Reprinted in *Puzzles and Epiphanies*, 1962.

——: "The case for William Golding", in *New York Review of Books*, 30 Apr. 1964.

LODGE, DAVID: "William Golding", in *Spectator*, 10 Apr. 1964.

MACLURE, MILLAR: "Allegories of Innocence", in *Dalhousie Review*, Summer 1960.

MARCUS, STEVEN: "The Novel Again", in *Partisan Review*, Spring 1962.

MORGAN, EDWIN: "*Pincher Martin* and *The Coral Island*", in *Notes & Queries*, Apr. 1960.

NIEMEYER, CARL: "*The Coral Island* revisited", in *College English*, Jan. 1961. (N)

OLDSEY, BERNARD S. AND WEINTRAUB, S.: "*Lord of the Flies*: Beelzebub revisited", in *College English*, Nov. 1963.

PAGE, NORMAN: "Lord of the Flies", in *Use of English*, Autumn 1964.

PEARSON, ANTHONY: "H. G. Wells and *Pincher Martin*", in *Notes & Queries*, Jul. 1965.

PETER, JOHN: "Fables of William Golding", in *Kenyon Review*, Fall 1957 (N)

PRITCHETT, V. S.: "Secret Parables", in *New Statesman*, 2 Aug. 1958. (N)

——: "God's Folly", in *New Statesman*, 10 Apr. 1964.

QUINN, MICHAEL: "An unheroic hero: William Golding's Pincher Martin", in *Critical Quarterly*, Autumn 1962.

REXROTH, K.: "William Golding", in *The Atlantic*, May 1965.

ROPER, D.: "Allegory and Novel in Golding's *The Spire*", in *Wisconsin Studies in Contemporary Literature*, Winter 1967.

ROSENFIELD, CLAIRE: "Men of smaller growth. A psychological analysis of William Golding's *Lord of the Flies*", in *Literature and Psychology*, Autumn 1961. (N)

SEYMOUR-SMITH, MARTIN: "Golding's Pyramid", in *Spectator*, 30 Jun. 1967.

SMITH, PETER-DUVAL: "Free Fall", in *New Statesman*, 24 Oct. 1959.

STERN, J.: "English schoolboys in the jungle", in *New York Times Book Review*, 23 Oct. 1955. (N)

TAYLOR, H. H.: "The case against William Golding's Simon-Piggy", in *Contemporary Review*, Sep. 1966.

TOWNSEND, R. C.: "*Lord of the Flies*: Fool's Gold?", in *Journal of General Education*, July 1964.

TREWIN, J. C.: "*The Brass Butterfly*", in *Illustrated London News*, 3 May 1958.

WAIN, JOHN: "Lord of the Agonies", in *Aspect*, April 1963.

WALTERS, MARGARET: "Two fabulists: Golding and Camus", in *Melbourne Critical Review*, No. 4. 1961. (N)
WASSERSTROM, W.: "Reason and reverence in art and science", in *Literature and Psychology*, Winter 1962.
WATSON, KENNETH: "*A reading of Lord of the Flies*", in *English*, Spring 1964.
WEBSTER, OWEN: "Living with chaos", in *Books and Art*, March 1958.
WEST, A.: "William Golding", in *New Yorker*, 30 Apr. 1960.
WHITEHEAD, JOHN: "A conducted tour to the Pyramid", in *London Magazine*, Jun. 1967.
WICKENDEN, DAN: "First Idyll, then Nightmare", in *New York Herald Tribune Book Review*, 23 Oct. 1955. (N)
YOUNG, WAYLAND: "Letter from London", in *Kenyon Review*, Summer 1957.

CAPRICORN TITLES

75. *Dewey,* FREEDOM & CULTURE. $1.45.
77. *Tasso,* JERUSALEM DELIVERED. $2.45.
78. *Fulford,* GEORGE THE FOURTH. $1.45.
81. *Fox,* GEORGE FOX'S JOURNAL. $1.95.
83. *Strachey,* EMINENT VICTORIANS. $1.65.
84. *Shaw,* ADVICE TO A YOUNG CRITIC. $1.45.
86. *Burton,* KAMA SUTRA. $.95.
87. *Kaster,* MYTHOLOGICAL DICTIONARY. $1.45.
88. *Rauch,* HISTORY OF THE NEW DEAL 1933-38. $1.95.
89. *Curnock,* JOURNAL OF JOHN WESLEY. $1.85.
90. *Ferrero,* SHORT HISTORY OF ROME—Vol. 1. $1.95.
91. *Ferrero,* SHORT HISTORY OF ROME—Vol. 2. $1.95.
94. *Symonds,* ITALIAN LITERATURE—Vol. 1. $1.85.
95. *Symonds,* ITALIAN LITERATURE—Vol. 2. $1.85.
97. *Strong,* HISTORY OF MODERN POLITICAL CONSTITUTION $1.95.
98. *Sterne,* A SENTIMENTAL JOURNEY. $1.25.
99. *Dick,* DIXIE FRONTIER. $1.95.
100. *Shaw,* TALES. $1.45.
101. *Ruchames,* THE ABOLITIONISTS. $1.65.
102. *Gramont,* AGE OF MAGNIFICENCE. $2.45.
105. *Chopin,* THE AWAKENING. $1.45.
106. *Taussig,* TARIFF HISTORY OF THE U.S. $2.45.
107. *Filler,* DEMOCRATS AND REPUBLICANS. $1.65.
108. *Adler,* SOCIAL INTEREST. $1.45.
111. *Dewey,* PHILOSOPHY, PSYCHOLOGY AND SOCIAL PRACTICE. $1.75.
112. *Redfield,* CAPRICORN RHYMING DICTIONARY. $1.75.
113. *Bruce,* SOCIAL LIFE IN OLD VIRGINIA. $2.25.
114. *Gregory,* OUR IRISH THEATRE. $1.95.
116. *Musil,* THE MAN WITHOUT QUALITIES. $1.85.
117. *Gregory,* OUR FACE FROM FISH TO MAN. $1.65.
118. *Antonius,* THE ARAB AWAKENING. $1.95.
119. *Burns,* MERRY MUSES OF CALEDONIA. $1.25.
120. *Viereck,* SHAME & GLORY OF INTELLECTUALS. $1.95.
121. *Good,* THE SCIENTIST SPECULATES. $1.95.
122. *Orgler,* ALFRED ADLER: MAN & WORK. $1.65.
123. *Thompson,* PEOPLE OF THE SERPENT. $1.65.
124. *Williams,* CAPITALISM & SLAVERY. $1.65.
125. *Archer,* GULISTAN OF SA'DI. $1.25.
126. *Wilstach,* CORRESPONDENCE OF ADAMS & JEFFERSON. $1.45.
127. *Christman,* PUBLIC PAPERS OF CHIEF JUSTICE WARREN. $2.25.
129. *Huxley,* AFFABLE SAVAGES. $2.45.
130. *Gielgud,* STAGE DIRECTIONS. $1.45.
132. *de Sade,* JUSTINE. $.95.
133. *Sidney,* ARCADIA & OTHER POETRY & PROSE. $1.75.
134. *Lebon,* INTRODUCTION TO HUMAN GEOGRAPHY. $1.45.
135. *Crone,* MAPS & THEIR MAKERS. $1.45.
136. *Potts,* COMEDY. $1.45.
137. *Jackson,* EIGHTEEN NINETIES. $2.25.
138. *Walzel,* GERMAN ROMANTICISM. $1.45.
139. *Smith,* CONGRESSMAN FROM MISSISSIPPI. $1.95.
140. *Olcott,* MYTHS OF THE SUN. $1.75.
141. *Brown,* MIND YOUR LANGUAGE. $1.25.

142. *Wooldridge & East,* SPIRIT & PURPOSE OF GEOGRAPHY. $1.45.
143. *Seton-Watson,* NEW IMPERIALISM. $1.45.
144. *Maude,* SOUTH ASIA. $1.45.
145. *Cranston,* WESTERN POLITICAL PHILOSOPHERS. $1.45.
146. *Agar,* PERILS OF DEMOCRACY. $1.25.
147. *Walston,* AGRICULTURE UNDER COMMUNISM. $1.25.
148. *Daniel,* MYTH OR LEGEND. $1.25.
149. *DeVoto,* MARK TWAIN IN ERUPTION. $2.45.
150. *Prabhabanda,* THE WISDOM OF GOD. $2.45.
151. *Malla,* THE ANANGA RANGA. $.95.
152. *Kraft-Ebing,* PSYCHOPATHIA SEXUALIS. $.95.
153. *Bahm,* PHILOSOPHY OF THE BUDDHA. $1.45.
154. *Diderot,* DIALOGUES. $1.65.
155. *Hadas,* GIBBON'S THE DECLINE AND FALL OF THE ROMAN EMPIRE. $1.95.
156. *Veblen,* VEBLEN ON MARX, RACE, SCIENCE AND ECONOMICS. $2.95.
157. *Veblen,* THE VESTED INTERESTS AND THE COMMON MAN. $1.65.
158. *Cruikshank,* THE CRUIKSHANK FAIRY BOOK. $1.45.
159. *Lowry,* HEAR US O LORD FROM HEAVEN THY DWELLING PLACE. $1.85.
160. *Adler,* STUDIES IN ANALYTICAL PSYCHOLOGY. $1.95.
162. *Matthews,* FUGGER NEWSLETTERS. $1.95.
164. *Marx,* REVOLUTION AND COUNTER-REVOLUTION. $1.95.

CAPRICORN GIANTS

201. *Hauser,* DIET DOES IT. $1.95.
202. *Moscati,* ANCIENT SEMITIC CIVILIZATIONS. $2.65.
204. *Brockelman,* HISTORY OF ISLAMIC PEOPLES. $2.65.
205. *Salter,* CONDITIONED REFLEX THERAPY. $1.95.
207. *Davis,* CORPORATIONS. $2.45.
208. *Rodman,* CONVERSATIONS WITH ARTISTS. $1.65.
209. *Falls,* GREAT WAR. $2.15.
210. *Pius II,* MEMOIRS OF A RENAISSANCE POPE. $1.95.
213. *Cournos,* TREASURY OF CLASSIC RUSSIAN LITERATURE. $2.45.
215. *Guerdan,* BYZANTIUM. $1.65.
217. *Bradford,* OF PLYMOUTH PLANTATION. $1.95.
218. *Taylor,* COURSE OF GERMAN HISTORY. $1.65.
220. *Shelby Little,* GEORGE WASHINGTON. $1.95.
221. *Peterson,* ANCIENT MEXICO. $1.95.
224. *Krafft-Ebing,* ABERRATIONS OF SEXUAL LIFE. $1.95.
227. *Ernst-Loth,* REPORT ON THE AMERICAN COMMUNIST. $1.45.
228. *Adler,* THE PROBLEM CHILD. $1.95.
233. *Barraclough,* ORIGINS OF MODERN GERMANY. $2.45.
235. *Skeat,* ETYMOLOGICAL DICTIONARY. $3.45.
236. *Hauser,* GAYLORD HAUSER COOK BOOK. $1.65.
237. *Fulop Miller,* THE JESUITS. $2.45.
239. *Blitzer,* COMMONWEALTH OF ENGLAND. $1.65.
240. *Wright,* GREAT AMERICAN GENTLEMAN. $1.95.

246. *Weinberg,* THE MUCKRAKERS. $2.45.
247. *Hays,* FROM APE TO ANGEL. $3.45.
248. *James,* ANCIENT GODS. $2.25.
249. *Green,* LUTHER AND THE REFORMATION. $1.65.
250. *Filler,* THE ANXIOUS YEARS. $2.95.
251. *Ehrlich,* EHRLICH'S BLACKSTONE: RIGHTS OF PERSONS, RIGHTS OF THINGS. $2.95.
252. *Ehrlich,* EHRLICH'S BLACKSTONE: PRIVATE WRONGS, PUBLIC WRONGS. $2.95.
254. *Collis,* QUEST FOR SITA. $1.75.
255. *Nabokov,* INVITATION TO A BEHEADING. $1.65.
256. *Wedeck,* PUTNAM'S DARK & MIDDLE AGES READER. $1.95.
257. *Perroy,* THE HUNDRED YEARS WAR. $2.65.
258. *George,* LONDON LIFE IN 18TH CENTURY. $2.95.
259. *Rankin,* THE AMERICAN REVOLUTION. $1.95.
260. STALIN'S CORRESPONDENCE WITH ROOSEVELT & TRUMAN. $1.95.
261. STALIN'S CORRESPONDENCE WITH CHURCHILL & ATTLEE. $2.25.
262. *White,* A PURITAN IN BABYLON. $2.45.
263. *Czernin,* VERSAILLES 1919. $2.45.
264. *Filler,* PRESIDENT SPEAKS. $2.25.
265. *Ming,* HISTORY OF CHINESE LITERATURE. $2.65.
266. *Mead,* CHANGING CULTURE OF AN INDIAN TRIBE. $2.75.
268. *Churchill,* YEARS OF ADVENTURE. $2.25.
269. *Churchill,* YEARS OF GREATNESS. $1.95.
270. *Trefousse,* COLD WAR. $1.95.
271. *Louys,* SONGS OF BILITIS. $1.25.
272. *Sydenham,* FRENCH REVOLUTION. $2.25.
273. *Ley,* WILLY LEY'S EXOTIC ZOOLOGY. $2.65.
274. *Thomson,* CHAMBERLAIN LETTERS. $2.45.
275. *Orem,* MONTESSORI HANDBOOK. $1.65.
276. *Jenkins,* ELIZABETH THE GREAT. $1.95.
277. *Simpson,* GEOGRAPHY OF EVOLUTION. $1.75.
278. *Brown & Harris,* RESTORATION THEATRE. $1.65.
279. *Brown & Harris,* JACOBEAN THEATRE. $1.65.
280. *Kim,* PATTERNS OF COMPETITIVE COEXISTENCE. $2.95.
281. *Reader,* LIFE IN VICTORIAN ENGLAND. $1.95.
282. *Tomkeieff,* LIFE IN NORMAN ENGLAND. $1.95.
283. *Chamberlin,* EVERYDAY LIFE IN RENAISSANCE TIMES. $1.95.
284. *White,* EVERYDAY LIFE IN ANCIENT EGYPT. $1.75.
285. *Millis,* ARMS AND MEN. $2.45.
286. *Laven,* RENAISSANCE ITALY. $1.85.
287. *Wish,* DIARY OF SAMUEL SEWALL. $1.95.
288. *Verrill,* AMERICA'S ANCIENT CIVILIZATIONS. $1.95.
289. *Lander,* WARS OF THE ROSES. $1.95.
290. *Orem,* MONTESSORI FOR THE DISADVANTAGED. $1.65.
291. *Shukman,* LENIN & THE RUSSIAN REVOLUTION. $1.65.
292. *Cavendish,* THE BLACK ARTS. $1.95.
293. *Burland,* GODS OF MEXICO. $1.85.
294. *O'Connor,* SHORT HISTORY OF IRISH LITERATURE. $1.85.
295. *Clarens,* ILLUSTRATED HISTORY OF THE HORROR FILM. $2.75.
296. *Nevins,* POLK: THE DIARY OF A PRESIDENT. $2.65.
297. *Ashbury,* THE BARBARY COAST. $2.25.
298. *Ashbury,* THE FRENCH QUARTER. $2.65.